London Eye

Tower Bridge

LY CIRCUS

The Shard

The Gherkin

ncras

MIND THE GAP

MIND THE GAP: A LONDON UNDERGROUND MISCELLANY

Copyright © Summersdale Publishers Ltd, 2013

Cover and illustrations by Kate Rochester / Pickled Ink
Illustrations copyright © 2012 Kate Rochester

Summersdale Publishers Ltd
46 West Street
Chichester
West Sussex
PO19 1RP
UK

www.summersdale.com

Printed and bound by CPI Group (UK) Ltd, Croydon CR0 4YY

ISBN: 978-1-84953-357-7

Substantial discounts on bulk quantities of Summersdale books are available to corporations, professional associations and other organisations. For details contact Nicky Douglas by telephone: +44 (0) 1243 756902, fax: +44 (0) 1243 786300 or email: nicky@summersdale.com

MIND THE GAP

A London Underground Miscellany

Emily Kearns

Illustrations by Kate Rochester

summersdale

For Elizabeth and Hugh Kearns

CONTENTS

INTRODUCTION

The first London Underground line opened in 1863, celebrating its 150th birthday in 2013. In the first year 40 million journeys were made on the system and that figure has now exceeded one billion. With 11 different lines serving 270 stations, over 249 miles (402 km) of track, on which up to 500 trains can be in operation during peak hours, it's a complex network that requires thousands of pairs of skilled hands to keep it going daily.

The birth of the Tube prompted the growth of London itself and, as the various lines sprawled out to the counties, so the capital followed. Sparking a veritable transport revolution, the Tube was the first underground railway the world had ever seen and hundreds of cities around the world have drawn inspiration from its strides forward in the engineering world.

This book takes a look at the history of the London Underground, and the remarkable people and determination behind its inception. It will touch on passenger behaviour, the trains themselves, what lurks beneath the surface and what the future holds for the network.

So, mind the doors, hold on tight, keep your feet off the seats and enjoy your journey.

1
THE FORMATION OF THE LONDON UNDERGROUND

PART ONE: 1825–1902

In the 1850s, new major mainline railway stations brought more and more people into the capital from the rest of the country. The roads in central London became chaotic and an underground railway seemed the perfect solution to combat the widespread congestion and rapidly increasing population of the city.

LONDON'S POPULATION GROWTH

1801 – 1.1 million
1851 – 2.4 million
1901 – 6.5 million
1951 – 8.2 million
2001 – 7.3 million
2011 – 8.2 million

The construction of the earliest parts of the Underground caused much disruption, as roads were trenched to make way for the new railway and slums demolished to create housing for its workers.

The cut-and-cover method – which involved digging up streets, laying tracks and covering with a brick-lined tunnel just below ground level – was originally used to build a transport network beneath the city, but it wasn't long before advancements in engineering spurred on the construction of a deep-level subterranean system.

The earliest Tube trains were steam-powered, filling underground stations with thick smoke and clouds of steam. Ventilation beneath the city streets became a major issue and shafts were sunk from ground level to promote airflow for the wellbeing of passengers. The shafts proved insufficient, however, and the smoke and steam continued to cause concern, despite the typically Victorian attitude of the Metropolitan Railway, which attempted to reassure passengers via advertising that the atmosphere was like 'a sort of health resort' for asthmatics.

From their first incarnations as steam trains, through the early electrified models, up to the occasionally shiny Tube trains we know today and the proposed driverless models of the future, engineering improvements seem to be constantly rumbling on the Underground. Then there is the seemingly never-ending, ever-growing network of tunnels and tracks connecting the pockets and corners of the capital further, thus cementing the facts that the London Underground has become essential to city life and is a constantly evolving machine.

Here we trace the history of the construction of a transport system that Londoners just can't live without.

UNDER THE RIVER

1825: Construction of the Thames Tunnel begins under the River Thames between Wapping and Rotherhithe. Using his patented tunnelling shield, Marc Isambard Brunel oversees progress of what is hoped will become a profitable business, aiding the transport of cargo from one side of the river to the other.

1827: Marc's son Isambard Kingdom Brunel is appointed resident engineer on the Thames Tunnel, and organises a lavish banquet beneath the river in an attempt to raise funds for the project and prove the construction is safe. The tunnel is far from finished, however, and is both dirty and rat-infested.

1828: The Thames Tunnel suffers from major flooding, and is bricked up and abandoned for seven years while Marc Isambard Brunel raises sufficient funds to continue work.

1843: Eighteen years after work began, the Thames Tunnel opens – but for the use of pedestrians only.

The first sub-river tunnel in the world stretches for 1,506 ft (406 m).

THE WORLD'S FIRST UNDERGROUND RAILWAY

1845: Charles Pearson, solicitor to the City of London, promotes the idea of an underground railway to transport both passengers and goods to the city centre. He claims going underground will solve overcrowding in the city, and his futuristic vision includes trains travelling through glass tunnels, pushed by compressed air.

1854: Permission is granted for the Metropolitan Railway to begin construction between Paddington and Farringdon, but it isn't until funding is secured in 1860 that the underground railway begins to take shape.

> A subterranean railway under London was awfully suggestive of dark, noisome tunnels, buried many fathoms deep beyond the reach of light of life; passages inhabited by rats, soaked with sewer drippings, and poisoned by the escape of gas mains.

It seemed an insult to common sense to suppose that people who could travel as cheaply to the city on the outside of a Paddington bus would ever prefer, as a merely quicker medium, to be driven amid palpable darkness through the foul subsoil of London.

The Times, 30 November 1861

1863: On 10 January the Metropolitan Railway goes down in the history books when it opens the first subterranean railway in the world. The initial stretch of track covers nearly four miles and more than 40,000 people use the railway on its first day.

1864: As the Hammersmith & City Railway is opened, London sees the first track extensions to Hammersmith and Kensington Olympia. The Metropolitan District Railway also steps up to begin the building of a line between Westminster and South Kensington.

1864: An idea is floated by both the Metropolitan and the Metropolitan District Railways to complete an Inner Circle line around the city centre. However, the two companies fall into a bitter rivalry and it takes 20 years to finish work on what eventually becomes known as the Circle line.

1865: The Thames Tunnel is bought by the East London Railway, which plans to convert it for railway use. The Metropolitan Railway sees an extension to Moorgate, which opens in December, and the Great Eastern Railway extends to Ongar – a station used primarily to transport produce from nearby farms into central London.

1867: The Edgware, Highgate & London Railway opens, five years after its inception, with a single-track line running from Finsbury Park to Edgware.

1868: Heading north out of the City, a short branch from Baker Street to Swiss Cottage is opened by the Metropolitan & St John's Wood Railway. The Metropolitan District Railway also begins to operate services between South Kensington and Westminster.

HEADING UNDER THE THAMES

1869: The Thames Tunnel finally becomes an essential part of the London Underground story as it opens for railway use, accommodating trains travelling on the East London Railway between New

Cross and Wapping. After descending into the tunnel, the steam trains have to work hard to climb uphill to the surface, producing more smoke than usual, and creating an altogether unpleasant atmosphere for passengers and railway workers. The lack of ventilation shafts in the tunnel only exacerbates this.

1870: After furthering its line from Gloucester Road to West Brompton, the Metropolitan District Railway completes work on its extension to Blackfriars.

1870: The Tower Subway opens and uses a cable-haul system to pull carriages between the Tower of London and Bermondsey. Measuring just 7 ft (2.1 m) in diameter, the tunnel is constructed using advanced techniques pioneered by South African-born engineer James Greathead and his tunnelling shield. The new and improved shield tunnels deeper than ever, as well as being cheaper and safer to use. Greathead's techniques are then used to dig many more of the deep-level Underground lines in London.

1871: The Metropolitan District Railway builds a route between Blackfriars and Mansion House, and the Brill Tramway, an extension of the Metropolitan Railway, opens.

1872: The Metropolitan District Railway and North London Railway start running an Outer Circle line service from Broad Street to Mansion House, via Willesden Junction, Addison Road and Earl's Court. The Metropolitan District Railway extends its service from Earl's Court to Kensington Olympia, while the Great Northern Railway pushes the Edgware, Highgate & London Railway route from East Finchley to High Barnet.

1873: The Edgware, Highgate & London Railway is further extended from Highgate to Alexandra Palace.

COMPLETING THE CIRCLE

1874: The Metropolitan District Railway introduces a route from Earl's Court to Hammersmith and plans for the Inner Circle line begin to take shape. This year sees the inception of the Metropolitan Inner Circle Completion Railway Company (MICCRC) to finish the job.

1876: Having laid tracks to Liverpool Street the previous year, the Metropolitan extends its line to Aldgate, and the East London Railway establishes a route between Whitechapel and Shoreditch.

1877: Eager to further connect with the ever-growing network, the Metropolitan District extends its line from Hammersmith to Ravenscourt Park, where it meets the London & South Western Railway, which continues on to Richmond.

1879: After its takeover of the MICCRC, the Metropolitan Railway lays tracks to Willesden Green; and the Metropolitan District pushes its services out from Turnham Green to Ealing Broadway.

DID YOU KNOW...?

In 1879 a chemist's located near the British Museum managed to sell up to 20 bottles a day of Metropolitan Mixture — a 'tonic' designed to help those suffering from ill health due to the atmosphere on the Metropolitan Railway.

1880: The Metropolitan alone is now experiencing 40 million journeys made annually. This year sees extensions by the Metropolitan District to Putney Bridge; the Metropolitan to Harrow-on-the-Hill; and the East London Railway to New Cross.

1882: The Metropolitan is extended from Aldgate to Tower of London.

COMPETITION RAGES ON

1883: As the two biggest railway companies in London continue to compete for dominance of the transport network, the Metropolitan District pushes further outside London with a service running to Windsor & Eton Central.

1884: The Inner Circle line – the first deep-level Underground line – is completed after 20 years in the making, and both the Metropolitan and Metropolitan District run services alongside each other. The two companies further their working relationship, heading east to St Mary's in Whitechapel, and making a connection with the East London Railway towards New Cross and New Cross Gate.

1885: While the Metropolitan opens a service to Pinner, the Metropolitan District closes its route from Ealing Broadway to Windsor & Eton Central after only two years.

1889: Wimbledon services commence from East Putney, thanks to the London & South Western Railway, and the Metropolitan adds a route to Chesham.

1890: The world's first deep-level electric railway is opened by the City & South London Railway, running from King William Street in the City, under the River Thames to Stockwell.

1898: The electrified Waterloo & City line opens between Waterloo and Bank, with services running between those two stations only to transport passengers beneath the River Thames.

1900: This year sees the birth of the 'Twopenny Tube' – in reference to its uniform fare of 2d – as the Central London Railway opens its line between Shepherd's Bush and Bank; the Prince of Wales (later Edward VII) cuts the ribbon at its opening.

1902: The Underground Electric Railways Company of London (also known as the Underground Group) is formed. Mergers will bring all railway companies – excluding the Metropolitan – under this banner by the time World War One breaks out.

TUBE STOP

MIND THE GAP

CHARING CROSS

The area surrounding this station was once a hamlet known as Charing – derived from the Anglo-Saxon word 'Cerring', meaning 'bend', which related to its position perched on the famous bend of the River Thames. The 'Cross' portion of the station's title dates back to the early 1290s, when King Edward I erected a wooden cross there in memory of his wife Eleanor of Castile.

PART TWO: 1905–2012

THE DAWN OF ELECTRIC RAILWAYS

1905: Railway companies are forced to improve the speed and efficiency of their services to encourage more Londoners to travel by Tube. This year sees a huge advance in the evolution of the network as the District, Circle and Metropolitan lines are electrified – 15 years after the opening of the electrified City & South London Railway. This development had been pioneered by American businessman and chairman of the Metropolitan District Electric Traction Company, Charles Tyson Yerkes, and the other lines quickly follow suit.

1906: The Baker Street & Waterloo Railway opens a route from Baker Street to Kennington Road (now Lambeth North) in March, and extends further to Elephant & Castle by August. The Great Northern, Piccadilly & Brompton Railway adds a section of track running between Hammersmith and Finsbury Park.

1907: The Charing Cross, Euston & Hampstead Railway opens from Charing Cross to Golders Green and Highgate. Albert Stanley (who would later become Lord Ashfield) is appointed general manager of the Underground Group and pushes for a recognisable symbol to bring the network together.

I have known a man, dying a long way from London, sigh queerly for a sight of the gush of smoke that, on the platform of the Underground, one may see, escaping in great woolly clots up a circular opening, by a grimy, rusted iron shield, into the dim upper light. He wanted to see it again as others have wished to see once more the Bay of Naples, the olive groves of Catania. But – alas perhaps – no man will ever see that sight again, for the Underground itself has been 'electrified'… and there is one of our glamours gone.

Ford Madox Hueffer –
England & the English: An Interpretation, 1907

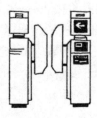

CREATING A BRAND

1908: The 'Underground' branding appears on stations belonging to the Underground Group and the famous roundel – then a simple red disc with a blue bar across it – makes its debut on publicity materials. Frank Pick is appointed head of publicity at the Underground Group and the first electric ticket-issuing machines are introduced.

1913: Both the Central London and City & South London Railways are absorbed into the Underground Group. The creative face of the network becomes a renewed focus as calligrapher Edward Johnston is commissioned to design a typeface for the Underground and the roundel.

1915: The Bakerloo line extends its services north-west to Queen's Park.

1920s: The Charing Cross, Euston & Hampstead and City & South London Railways are merged to form what, in 1937, would become known as the Northern line. Improvement works see the Golders Green branch extended to Edgware and the southern arm reaching down to Morden.

FRANK PICK TAKES CHARGE

1928: Frank Pick is appointed managing director of the Underground Group and commissions Charles Holden to design Underground stations that reflect the modern, progressive direction of the capital's transport system.

1931: Holden's first station commissioned by Pick opens at Sudbury Town on the Piccadilly line. It is sleek, modern, understated and unlike anything Britain has ever seen.

1933: The Underground Group and Metropolitan Railway become part of the newly formed London Passenger Transport Board (also known as London Transport), which takes control of all railway, bus, tram, trolleybus and coach services in the capital.

1940: As World War Two rages, Underground platforms are used as air-raid shelters and many deep-level stations house those seeking refuge from the Blitz come nightfall (see Chapter 7).

POST-WAR LONDON

1946–1949: The Central line takes shape as it branches out to east London and beyond, introducing services that make use of Great Western and Eastern Railway routes.

1947: Prime Minister Clement Attlee's vision for Britain comes into play with his programme of nationalisation. Along with the coal, and eventually gas and electricity industries, the country's railways are all taken under state control, and the London Passenger Transport Board's responsibilities are passed over to the London Transport Executive, part of the British Transport Commission.

1952: This year sees the first aluminium train enter service on the District line. 'Route C' is also proposed and will eventually become the Victoria line, but there is to be a long wait for investment.

1957: Upon electrification, the Central line takes over the shuttle service that serves Epping to Ongar from British Rail.

1959: The South Acton branch of the District line closes to the public this year after 79 years. The branch remains in use for goods trains passing through until the mid 1960s.

1962: Funding is finally approved for 'Route C', 10 years after the service was originally proposed.

ALL CHANGE

1963: The London Transport Executive becomes the London Transport Board and reports directly to the Minister of Transport. Only a few years later, in 1967, London Transport is transferred to the Greater London Council.

1968–1969: The Queen opens the Victoria line, and its first services operate between Walthamstow Central and Highbury & Islington. The line is then extended to Warren Street and on to Victoria shortly afterwards.

1971: The Victoria line is extended south to Brixton and, in the same year, a 'Fleet' line (which upon inception will be named the Jubilee) is authorised.

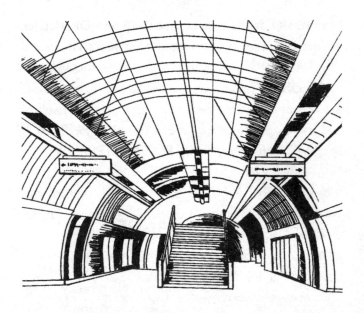

1977: The Queen opens Heathrow Central Station, which serves Terminals 1, 2 and 3 of Heathrow Airport.

1979: The Prince of Wales opens the Jubilee line and the new service takes over the operation of the Stanmore branch from Bakerloo.

1981: Labour gains control of the Greater London Council and, as leader, Ken Livingstone introduces a 'Fares Fair' policy using government subsidies, reducing ticket prices and introducing zonal fares. The reduced fares don't last the year, but the flat fares within zones do and the same structure is still in place today.

1983: Dot-matrix displays showing train destinations are introduced on platforms this year. Margaret Thatcher and the Conservatives win the General Election and promise to abolish the Greater London Council.

1984: London Regional Transport is created and takes over the running of the Underground from the Greater London Council. One-person operation is phased in on Tube trains, as guards are withdrawn and train drivers are responsible for operating the doors. This year sees construction begin on the Docklands Light Railway.

1985: This year sees the abolition of the Greater London Council, with the Conservative government arguing the boroughs can oversee operations much more efficiently.

1986: The Piccadilly line is extended to serve the newly opened, £200 million Terminal 4 at Heathrow Airport.

1987: The first stretch of the DLR is officially opened by the Queen. The original line runs east from Tower

Gateway, splitting at Poplar to head north to Stratford and south to Island Gardens.

1991: The DLR Bank extension opens this year, as does Canary Wharf station, and the line gains a new fleet of stock.

1993: Work starts this year to extend the Jubilee line from Green Park to Stratford. Prime Minister John Major drives the first pile at Canary Wharf as construction gets under way.

1994: On-the-spot penalty fares of £10 are introduced for fare evaders and London Underground takes control of the Waterloo & City line.

1999: The Jubilee line ploughs east to Stratford as the next phase of the £3.5 billion extension project opens.

2000: Transport for London (TfL) is formed and comes under the authority of the London Mayor, Ken Livingstone.

2003: London Underground is restructured, becomes part of Transport for London and, in doing so, is semi-privatised by way of a public-private partnership. This transfers all maintenance responsibilities for the track, signalling and stations to three private backers.

2007: This year sees the closure of the East London line and the Thames Tunnel to allow maintenance work on the river passage and link the Underground rail service to the London Overground in preparation for the London 2012 Olympics.

2008: The Piccadilly line extends to Heathrow Airport's newly opened Terminal 5. Wood Lane station is resurrected this year on the Hammersmith & City line, within close proximity to the station of the same name that was closed in 1959.

2009: Construction begins on Crossrail, the major route that will run from Berkshire to Essex, via the depths of the city. This year sees the opening of the DLR extension to Woolwich Arsenal, as well as the revamped Tower Gateway station.

2011: The Thames Tunnel and the new London Overground extension reopen after four years of regeneration, and the DLR Stratford International to Canning Town route opens in plenty of time for the London 2012 Olympic Games.

2012: The Underground carries more than 60 million passengers during the Olympics – more than at any time in its history over such a short period – and the Tube Upgrade project continues to increase capacity for ever-growing demand.

WHAT'S IN A NAME?

Baker Street & Waterloo Railway – quickly dubbed the **Bakerloo** line in 1906

Central London Railway – rebranded the **Central** line in 1937

Inner Circle – renamed the **Circle** line in 1949

Metropolitan District Railway – became known as the **District** line in 1868

City & South London Railway and Charing Cross, Euston & Hampstead Railway – linked and then rebranded as the **Northern** line in 1937

Great Northern, Piccadilly & Brompton Railway – renamed the **Piccadilly** line in 1906

TUBE STOP

SEVEN SISTERS

This area of north London takes it name from seven elm trees planted in a circle several hundred years ago, which stood there until the 1830s. Legend has it the trees were planted by seven sisters who lived there. The tradition continued as fresh trees were planted in 1886, 1955 and 1997, each time by a set of seven sisters.

2
OLD LINES, NEW LINES

From the introduction of the Metropolitan Railway in 1863, the London Underground network has branched out to sprawl all over the city and beyond, linking central London with Greater London and clinging to the outskirts of Buckinghamshire, Hampshire and Essex.

In order to create a user-friendly aid to the transport system, in 1933 electrical draftsman Harry Beck designed the first diagrammatic Underground map, the shape of which was based on a circuit board, offering a clear representation of the network. The map proved so popular it has been used and added to ever since.

It is only in recent times that the map has faced criticism for leading passengers on longer journeys than is always necessary. Zhan Guo, professor of urban planning at New York University, conducted a survey among London commuters and, upon assessing his findings, claimed they even trusted the map over their own experiences.

He said: 'The map effect is almost two times more influential than the actual travel time. In other words, Underground passengers trust the Tube map (two times) more than their own travel experience with the system. The map effect decreases when passengers become more familiar with the system but is still greater than the effect of the actual experience, even for passengers who use the Underground five days or more per week.'

Psychologist Dr Max Roberts, a self-confessed Tube fanatic, has given the iconic map several makeovers, including laying it out in a geographically accurate, pre-Beck style. It is widely agreed, however, that Beck's map proves the most easily navigable.

Bill Bryson, in *Notes From a Small Island*, offers a trick to play on friends visiting London. Tell them to travel from Bank to Mansion House, he says, and they'll take the Central line to Liverpool Street, followed by a Circle line train for five stops to reach their destination, but they will find themselves just 200 ft from the point at which they started!

Bakerloo

Colour: Brown
Opened: 1906
Originally known as: Baker Street & Waterloo Railway
Runs from: Harrow & Wealdstone to Elephant & Castle
Distance covered: 14.5 miles (23.2 km)
No. of stops: 25
Longest stop: Harrow & Wealdstone to Kenton –
1.08 miles (1.74 km)
Shortest stop: Charing Cross to Embankment –
0.23 miles (0.37 km)

Facts:

- After opening, it was quickly nicknamed the Bakerloo line by the *Evening News,* and rumour has it the route was created to swiftly transport London businessmen to Lord's Cricket Ground and back.

- Baker Street has more platforms running Tube trains than any other on the network – two for the Bakerloo line, two for the Circle, two for the Jubilee and four for the Metropolitan.

Central

Colour: Red
Opened: 1900
Originally known as: Central London Railway
Runs from: West Ruislip or Ealing Broadway to Epping
Distance covered: 46 miles (74 km)
No. of stops: 49
Longest stop: Mile End to Stratford – 1.76 miles (2.83 km)
Shortest stop: Holborn to Chancery Lane – 0.25 miles (0.40 km)

Facts:

⊖ The Central line is the longest line on the network. Should you be inclined, you could make the longest journey possible on the Tube without stopping – hopping on at West Ruislip and off at Epping, travelling 34.1 miles (54.9 km).

⊖ Redbridge boasts the shallowest platforms on the Underground, at just 26 ft (7.9 m) below the road surface, and the Central line also boasts the shortest escalator, at Stratford, reaching just 13.5 ft (4.1 m).

Circle

Colour: Yellow
Opened: 1884
Originally known as: Inner Circle line
Runs from: Hammersmith to Edgware Road
Distance covered: 17 miles (27 km)
No. of stops: 36
Longest stop: Farringdon to King's Cross St Pancras –
1.15 miles (1.85 km)
Shortest stop: Mansion House to Cannon Street –
0.19 miles (0.31 km)

Facts:

- The Circle line shares almost its entire route with one or more of the District, Hammersmith & City and Metropolitan lines. The only stretches of track used solely by Circle line trains are between High Street Kensington and Gloucester Road, and Aldgate and Minories Junction (east of Tower Hill).

- Circle line trains were considered 'guests' on its various stretches belonging to other lines – until the Tube upgrade in 2008 allowed its trains more freedom in entering and exiting the circle.

District

Colour: Green
Opened: 1868
Originally known as: Metropolitan District Railway
Runs from: Ealing Broadway, Richmond or Wimbledon to Kensington (Olympia), Edgware or Upminster
Distance covered: 40 miles (64 km)
No. of stops: 60
Longest stop: Elm Park to Dagenham East – 1.47 miles (2.37 km)
Shortest stop: Cannon Street to Mansion House – 0.19 miles (0.31 km)

Facts:

⊖ Earl's Court was the first station on the Underground to have escalators installed. In 1911, it allegedly employed a one-legged man to ride them all day to prove their safety. Despite there since being doubt cast over this story, a tiny model of 'Bumper Harris' by an escalator can still be found at the Transport Museum's Acton Depot.

⊖ The District line is one of the most complex on the network and is therefore one of the most difficult to operate. Earl's Court has become the hub of the line from which all destinations can be reached.

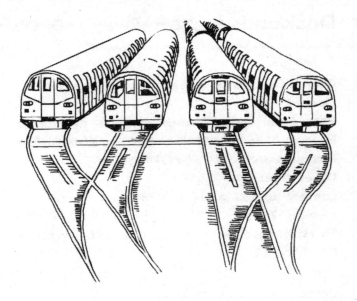

TUBE TRIVIA

Mansion House and South Ealing are the only station names to contain all five vowels.

Docklands Light Railway

Colour: Cyan (with a white stripe down the middle)
Opened: 1987
Runs from: Tower Gateway and Bank to Stratford International, Beckton, Woolwich Arsenal and Lewisham
Distance covered: 24 miles (39 km)
No. of stops: 45
Longest stop: King George V to Woolwich Arsenal – 1.5 miles (2.4 km)
Shortest stop: West India Quay to Canary Wharf – 0.12 miles (0.20 km)

Facts:

- The DLR was one of Britain's first light rail systems, the others being the Tyne & Wear Metro and the Manchester Metrolink.

- According to TfL, it boasts one of the 'safest and most advanced automatic train control systems in the world'.

- It was the first fully accessible railway in the UK, boasting step-free entrances to and exits from all trains and stations.

East London

Colour: Orange
Opened: 1869 (became part of the London Underground in 1933; closed in 2007)
Originally known as: East London Railway
Ran from: Shoreditch to New Cross and New Cross Gate
Distance covered: 4.6 miles (7.4 km)
No. of stops: 9
Longest stop: New Cross to Surrey Quays – 1.41 miles (2.27 km)
Shortest stop: Canada Water to Rotherhithe – 0.2 miles (0.32 km)

Facts:

- The oldest section of the Underground – the Grade II-listed Thames Tunnel linking Wapping with Rotherhithe – was used on the East London line route.

- The line closed in 2007 as part of TfL's £10 billion investment programme and was reopened in 2010 as part of the London Overground network.

Hammersmith & City

Colour: Pink
Opened: 1864 (branded a separate line in 1990)
Runs from: Hammersmith to Barking
Distance covered: 16.5 miles (26.5 km)
No. of stops: 29
Longest stop: East Ham to Barking – 1.42 miles (2.29 km)
Shortest stop: Tied between Goldhawk Road to Shepherd's Bush Market, Farringdon to Barbican and Moorgate to Liverpool Street – 0.32 miles (0.51 km)

Facts:

⊖ The section of track between Hammersmith and Farringdon was originally constructed to accommodate the broad-gauge trains operated in the nineteenth century by the Great Western Railway. Extra room between the tracks and in tunnels can be seen today, as the newer train models require less space.

⊖ The Hammersmith & City line was depicted on Tube maps in the Metropolitan line's magenta, until it was branded as a separate line in 1990 and duly shown on Underground maps in pink.

Jubilee

Colour: Silver
Opened: 1979
Runs from: Stanmore to Stratford
Distance covered: 22.5 miles (36.2 km)
No. of stops: 27
Longest stop: Kingsbury to Wembley Park – 1.77 miles (2.85 km)
Shortest stop: Waterloo to Southwark – 0.27 miles (0.44 km)

Facts:

⊖ The Jubilee is the only line that connects with all other lines on the Underground.

⊖ The line was named and coloured so to commemorate Queen Elizabeth II's Silver Jubilee, which was celebrated in 1977.

⊖ Despite being the youngest of the London Underground lines, the Jubilee serves stations that originally opened more than a hundred years ago.

⊖ The Jubilee line extension from central London to Greenwich was one of the world's most expensive transport projects. The construction amounted to around £3.3 billion – so each mile of the 10-mile track cost £330 million.

Metropolitan

Colour: Magenta
Opened: 1863
Originally known as: Metropolitan District Railway
Runs from: Amersham, Chesham, Watford or Uxbridge to Aldgate
Distance covered: 41.4 miles (66.7 km)
No. of stops: 34
Longest stop: Chesham to Chalfont & Latimer – 3.89 miles (6.26 km)
Shortest stop: Tied between Liverpool Street to Moorgate and Barbican to Farringdon – 0.32 miles (0.51 km)

Facts:

⊖ The Metropolitan District was the world's first subterranean railway – even though just 6 miles (9.7 km) of the line's 41.4 miles (66.7 km) are underground.

⊖ Amersham is the Tube station that sits the highest above sea level, at 490 ft (147 m).

⊖ The Metropolitan line boasts the longest distance between any two adjacent stations – Chesham and Chalfont & Latimer, which are 3.89 miles (6.26 km) apart.

DID YOU KNOW...?

When it first opened, the City & South London Railway was dubbed the 'Sardine Box Railway' by *Punch* magazine.

TUBE TRIVIA

The phrase 'Mind the gap' originated on the Northern line, where the gap between the train and the curved platform at Embankment was particularly large.

Northern

Colour: Black
Opened: 1890
Originally known as: City & South London Railway and Charing Cross, Euston & Hampstead Railway
Runs from: Edgware, High Barnet or Mill Hill East to Morden
Distance covered: 36 miles (58 km)
No of stops: 50
Longest stop: High Barnet to Totteridge & Whetstone – 1.53 miles (2.46 km)
Shortest stop: Charing Cross to Embankment – 0.23 miles (0.37 km)

Facts:

⊖ Hampstead swipes the trophy for the deepest station, plummeting 192 ft (58.5 m).

⊖ The longest journey you can make on the Tube – always staying underground – is on the Northern line between Morden and East Finchley, via the City branch, covering 17.25 miles (27.8 km).

⊖ The deepest point below ground level – 221 ft (67.4 m) – on the Underground network is on the Northern line at Holly Bush Hill, Hampstead.

Piccadilly

Colour: Dark blue
Opened: 1906
Originally known as: Great Northern, Piccadilly & Brompton Railway
Runs from: Heathrow Terminal 5 and Uxbridge to Cockfosters
Distance covered: 44 miles (71 km)
No of stops: 53
Longest stop: Hatton Cross to Hounslow West – 1.81 miles (2.91 km)
Shortest stop: Leicester Square to Covent Garden – 0.16 miles (0.25 km)

Facts:

⊖ Upon opening, the line quickly became known as the Piccadilly line, despite *The Times* newspaper attempting to get the title 'Hammercross' to catch on – the Piccadilly originally ran from Hammersmith to King's Cross – à la Bakerloo.

⊖ Arsenal is the only station on the network to actually be named after a football club. After moving from Woolwich to Gillespie Road in 1913, the club grew in prominence and the station was renamed in 1932.

Victoria

Colour: Light blue
Opened: 1968
Runs from: Brixton to Walthamstow Central
Distance covered: 13 miles (21 km)
No of stops: 16
Longest stop: Seven Sisters to Finsbury Park – 1.96 miles (3.15 km)
Shortest stop: King's Cross St Pancras to Euston – 0.46 miles (0.74 km)

Facts:

- The Victoria was the first new underground line to be introduced across central London for 60 years and was the first to venture into south London since the Northern line extended to Morden in 1926.

- When it came to naming the Victoria line, other suggestions were 'Walvic' (Walthamstow to Victoria) and 'Viking' (Victoria to King's Cross).

Waterloo & City

Colour: Turquoise
Opened: 1898
Runs from: Waterloo to Bank
Distance covered: 1.47 miles (2.37 km)
No of stops: 2
Time it takes to travel from end to end: 4 minutes

Facts:

- The Waterloo & City is the shortest line on the network, running between just two stops – Bank and Waterloo.

- Often referred to as 'the Drain', as the line passes under the River Thames, it was designed to transport commuters from one side of the City to the other.

TUBE STOP

MIND THE GAP

MOORGATE

This central London station's name is derived from the Moor Gate that was built into the city wall in 1415. The gate led to a patch of marshy ground known as Moorfields, and was designed to improve passage to both Islington and Hoxton. The gate was demolished in 1762 and the name passed on to Moorgate Street, which was built in the 1830s to connect the area with London Bridge.

3

THE TRAINS

From the early steam locomotive-hauled carriage set-up to the more efficient modern examples we know and love, the Tube train has steadily evolved over the course of the Underground's history. The electrified models were built to last, with some trundling the network for decades before being removed from service and replaced with updated versions.

Here we take a look at the stock more recently used on the system – so pay attention and spot the train you've no doubt had the pleasure to be transported upon.

We worked ten-hour days, eight times round the Circle. In the summer you could hardly breathe going through the tunnels, it was so hot… I'd shovel about two hundredweight of coal in a day's work. It was a dirty, hot, sweaty job.

George Spiller, District line fireman, 1900s

IN ORDER OF APPEARANCE...

A stock

⊖ The subsurface A60s were first introduced on the Metropolitan line in 1961, followed by the A62s a year later. Many of these trains served on the line for an impressive 50 years.

⊖ Remarkably durable, and sporting a design that has little changed over the decades, these trains took over from the outdated slam-door steam locomotives still operating at the time on the Metro-land edges of the Metropolitan line.

⊖ These trains operated as four-car services on the Chesham arm of the line, but were formed of eight cars throughout London.

⊖ Taken out of service in 2010.

1967 stock

⊖ Served on the Victoria line from its opening in 1968.

- Automatically driven and comprised of eight carriages.

- First appearance of wraparound windscreens and panoramic side windows.

- Interior dominated by plastic, rather than the wood cladding and painted surfaces that were the norm on previous models.

1972 MkI & MkII stock

⊖ Just 30 1972 MkI Tube trains were produced to serve the Piccadilly line upon its extension in the 1970s.

⊖ Much the same as 1967 stock, but with fewer carriages and equipped for two-person operation.

⊖ The MkII trains ran on the Northern line, then provided the initial fleet for the Jubilee line when it opened in 1979, and were then transferred to the Bakerloo line.

⊖ MkI stock taken out of service in November 1998.

1973 stock

⊖ First Tube trains to have extended carriages and all-electric control of air brakes.

⊖ Featured six carriages rather than the standard seven, due to their length.

⊖ Brought into operation on the Piccadilly line to serve Heathrow Airport, with designated space for luggage and more room in general by fitting longitudinal seats.

DID YOU KNOW...?

Face on, subsurface (cut and cover) stock measures 12.1 ft (3.7 m) from top to bottom and 9.7 ft (2.9 m) across, while Tube stock is dwarfed in comparison at 9.5 ft (2.9 m) by 8.5 ft (2.6 m).

C stock

- Subsurface stock first introduced in 1969 on the Circle, District and Hammersmith & City lines.

- Each car features four double doorways for efficient boarding.

- Formed of six carriages, these are the shortest trains operating in central London, owing to short platforms at some Circle line stations.

D stock

- Subsurface stock first introduced in 1980 on the District line and used on the East London line in the early 1980s.

- Design based on the 1973 stock.

- Features six carriages and single-leaf doors, which leads to less efficient boarding when compared with other models.

1992 stock

- Introduced one-person operation to the Central line.

- Features eight cars of standard length – rather than extended carriages à la 1973 stock – due to tight curves on the route.

- Wider passenger doors and longitudinal seats.

- These are of monocoque construction – a technique that allows the outer shell, rather than the structural frame, to support the load, as was the case with previous Tube trains.

1995 & 1996 stock

- Ordered for the opening of the Jubilee line extension, the 1995 and 1996 Tube stock has all the benefits of the 1992 stock, but are externally more conventional to match the older models on the route.

⊖ Originally comprising six carriages, this was upped to seven in 2005 to cater to demand.

2009 stock

⊖ Designed for the Victoria line, these were the first new models to be brought in since it opened in 1968.

⊖ Larger than standard Tube trains, owing to the wider tunnels on this route.

⊖ Formed of eight carriages to maximise capacity and efficiency.

⊖ Superior acceleration and deceleration.

⊖ Mod cons, such as advanced passenger information systems.

S stock

⊖ Subsurface stock first used on the Metropolitan line in 2010, these trains replaced the trusty A stock and were designed to increase capacity.

⊖ Through walkway between carriages appears for the first time – allowing passengers to move freely and providing extra space.

⊖ Features a modernised passenger-information system detailing local attractions as well as the standard journey particulars.

⊖ There are plans for the S stock trains to be rolled out across other subsurface routes by 2015.

RETIRING TO THE ISLE OF WIGHT

You'd be forgiven for assuming old Tube stock is quietly led to the scrapheap when it's no longer needed, but this isn't always the case. The trains used on the Island line on the Isle of Wight spent their glory years (more than 50 of them) serving the Northern line, before they retired in 1989 to spend their final days as somewhat sleepier two-carriage services on the 8-mile Ryde Pier Head to Shanklin route. After a refreshing of the interior, the wood-panelled 1930s trains exude vintage-transport chic and are the oldest in service in the country.

I like the Tube more than the New York Subway – you've got cushioned seats.

Neil Patrick Harris, actor

WHAT ARE YOU SITTING ON?

Ever wondered what happens to the delightfully garish, bristly moquette fabric on Tube seats once they are reupholstered with new designs? Well, wonder no more!

In the 1990s design agency Creatively Recycled Empire (now Above+Below London) worked alongside London Transport over a period of seven years, recycling a whopping 2 tonnes of fabric from 5,833 old Tube-train seats. The iconic patterns were given a new lease of life and came back in the guise of cushions and footwear, which can be found in the London Transport Museum shop or at:

www.ltmuseumshop.com
www.urbanremade.com
www.aboveandbelowlondon.com

The LTM shop also offers classic moquette designs fashioned into wallets, key rings, footrests, doormats and much more.

TUBE STOP

COVENT GARDEN

In the 1400s, the area surrounding Covent Garden belonged to the Benedictines of Westminster Abbey and was referred to as the 'Convent Garden'. In the 1600s the area was redeveloped and, as a town-planning experiment, saw the creation of the first town square in the country.

4

PEOPLE OF THE TUBE

Behind every great invention is a great mind – and the London Underground is no exception. In this case, it took several progressive thinkers and innovative designers to produce the service that we know and (generally) love today. The very notion that trains could run underneath the streets of London took a confident soul to present it. Charles Pearson, the brains behind the initial idea, may have imagined a futuristic form of transportation travelling through glass tunnels, pushed by the force of compressed air, which was not exactly what he got, but it was certainly the start of something quite revolutionary.

From Pearson, who sadly died mere weeks before the opening of his proposed railway, to those who led the growth of the network and chaired the many guises of London Transport, to the creative minds that concocted the brand now synonymous with London and devised the architecturally iconic stations perched on many a London street corner – here we take a look at the key figures who contributed to the Tube's success.

A TRANSPORT REVOLUTION

CHARLES PEARSON, 1793–1862

Touting a vision for a subterranean railway to rid the City streets of congestion, solicitor to the City of London Charles Pearson proposed that 'trains in drains' running beneath the streets could be the answer. In 1845, just 15 years after the first steam-train passenger services began, Pearson helped persuade the House of Commons to pass a bill to allow sub-surface tracks to be laid from Paddington to Farringdon. He also became heavily involved in recruiting private investors to fund the project and promoted the underground railway as a mode of transport all classes could afford.

JAMES HENRY GREATHEAD, 1844–1896

South African-born James Henry Greathead developed a tunnelling shield that became integral to the construction of the deep-level Tube lines. Consisting of an iron cylinder fitted with screw jacks, which enabled it to inch forward while workmen lined the tunnel behind it with cast-iron segments, squirting concrete in between the panels to create a watertight seal, the shield made tunnelling safer and cheaper. Greathead's tunnelling shield allowed lines to be dug deeper than ever, with no disruption to the city streets above. He left a true mark on the London Underground system and held chief engineering positions with many of the railway companies over the course of his life.

CHARLES TYSON YERKES, 1837–1905

In 1898, American businessman Charles Tyson Yerkes took a chance and invested in the Metropolitan District Railway, which was in poor condition and in urgent need of updating. Taking a great interest in other as-yet-unfinished railway projects in subterranean London, Yerkes went on to oversee the building of the Charing Cross, Euston & Hampstead Railway (now part of the Northern line), pushing for the route to be extended to Golders Green, which was then open fields, but ripe for development. Going on to form the Metropolitan District Electric Traction Company, he acquired funding from overseas and took control of the railway companies, along with the Bakerloo line, bringing them all under the same umbrella and thus becoming instrumental in the linking of the various services to create much of the network in operation today. Yerkes won a lengthy battle to convince his backers that electrification would save the Tube and, shortly before his death in 1905, he saw his goal realised.

BRANDING THE TUBE

ALBERT STANLEY (LORD ASHFIELD), 1874–1948

British-American Albert Stanley was appointed general manager of the Underground Electric Railways Company of London in 1907, when the company was swiftly heading for financial ruin and in desperate need of help. Stanley's experience heading up the Detroit Street Railways Company in the US made him a prime candidate. His task was to reverse the UERL's fortunes and essentially save the Tube from closure; Yerkes had helped to grow the network, with three lines constructed in a short space of time, but this had left the company with large debts. Stanley duly set about ramping up advertising and public relations to improve the UERL's position, working with Frank Pick to create a brand for the Underground and persuading the public to use the Tube to pursue leisure activities. His methods were highly successful in turning around the company's fortunes. In 1910, Stanley was appointed managing director and persuaded American investors to back the merger of several of the railway companies; further consolidation followed in 1912, providing the roots of London Transport. After being knighted in 1914, Stanley assumed a brief position at the War Office and a stint as MP for Ashton-under-Lyne, before returning to the Underground Group and eventually orchestrating the formation of the London Passenger Transport Board. Stanley's memorial at TfL's 55 Broadway headquarters says simply: 'Creator of London Transport'.

FRANK PICK, 1878–1941

Working under Albert Stanley at the UERL, Frank Pick's contribution to the development of London Underground's corporate identity set the tone for the future. Pick introduced the famous roundel to display station names clearly and bring the entire network under one brand. He then commissioned calligrapher Edward Johnston to come up with the famous 'Underground' lettering and called on Harry Beck to redesign the Tube map in a user-friendly format. Given the task of encouraging Londoners to use the

Underground outside of peak hours, he arranged for posters detailing recreational activities to be placed in stations around the City. While Tube-station walls had once been a clumsy mess of jumbled advertisements, some obscuring the station names themselves, Pick set about standardising poster sizes and arranging the control of their placement on station walls. Pick also pushed for the construction of routes further into the suburbs and enlisted architect Charles Holden to design many of the stations. Pick's contribution was well recognised but he declined offers of both a knighthood and a peerage.

Frank Pick

Charles Pearson

Harry Beck

THE ART OF THE MATTER

With the need to encourage more non-commuters to use the Tube, Frank Pick set about commissioning artists to design posters advertising recreational activities and tourist attractions. He enlisted Edward McKnight Kauffer and Elijah Cox, among others, to create colourful designs, thereby introducing variety and enticing different groups of society to use the Tube to travel across London to visit historic houses, museums, parks and cinemas. The posters were given pride of place in stations and attached to illuminated boards so they couldn't be missed.

ESSENTIAL ELEMENTS OF DESIGN

LESLIE GREEN, 1875–1908

London architect Leslie Green was responsible for the design of many of the Tube stations dotted around the capital. Any Londoner will be familiar with the oxblood-red glazed terracotta block facades of stations such as Covent Garden, Russell Square, Camden Town and Leicester Square, to name but a few, that have become iconic. Large semicircular windows and wide entrances allowed light to pour into the ticket halls, and the stations were built with flat roofs to enable offices to be constructed above. Green took much inspiration from the Art Nouveau he was exposed to while studying in Paris early on in his career. Standing the test of time, many of Green's original stations remain and, although most of his classic tiling designs at platform level have been modernised over the years, a few stations have reproduced the original patterns. Green contracted tuberculosis in 1908 – shortly after many of his iconic stations opened – and died at the age of 33.

CHARLES HOLDEN, 1875–1960

When Frank Pick appointed Charles Holden to design a clutch of station buildings for the new suburban lines, little did he realise the iconic status the art deco constructions would go on to attain. Holden had designed several Tube stations prior to Pick's appointment, but his buildings that followed took on a fresh new direction, the first being Sudbury Town on the Piccadilly line, which opened in 1931. His designs were unique to Britain at the time: modern and sleek, yet somewhat timeless. However, Holden was also concerned with the functionality of the buildings, concentrating on their efficiency in terms of passenger flow and how rainwater might clean the exteriors. He was a modest fellow, once referring to one of his creations as simply 'a brick box with a concrete lid'. He also believed architecture was a collaborative process and graciously declined a knighthood for his efforts – twice.

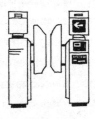

TUBE STOP

MIND THE GAP

SWISS COTTAGE

The area around Swiss Cottage takes its name from a chalet-style watering hole in the area called the Swiss Tavern. The tavern was built in 1803 on land formerly occupied by a toll house and later changed its name to Ye Olde Swiss Cottage to tie in with the newly christened area. The pub was rebuilt in the 1960s and sits on Finchley Road.

5

LEARNING TO LOVE
THE TUBE

Despite the disruption caused throughout London while the Metropolitan Railway cut-and-cover lines were being built, the introduction of this new transport system essentially brought the city together. It also proved an altogether socially egalitarian milestone, as people from all classes could afford to travel by Tube – which had not been the case with the omnibus surface transport trundling the streets of London previously.

This was a transport system that helped shape the city above it. London was cramped and its roads were heavily congested, but the Underground helped take traffic off the streets, offered rapid travel from one side of the densely populated metropolis to the other and would eventually contribute to the growth of London as it sprawled towards county lines.

There's no security, or peace and tranquillity, except underground. And then, if your ideas get larger and you want to expand – why, a dig and a scrape and there you are!

Badger, *The Wind in the Willows*,
Kenneth Grahame, 1908

FIRST JOURNEYS

Just two weeks after the grand opening of the Metropolitan Railway, diarist William Hardman wrote kindly of his first trip 'down the Drain', saying: 'We experienced no disagreeable odour, beyond the smell common to tunnels. The carriages hold 10 persons, with divided seats and are lighted by gas; they are also so lofty that a six-footer may stand erect with his hat on.'

However, some 25 years later, in 1887, American journalist R. D. Blumenfeld (who went on to become editor of the *Daily Express*) was not quite so taken with the system: 'I had my first experience of Hades to-day,' he said, 'and if the real thing is to be like that, I shall never again do anything wrong.' He described the atmosphere as 'a mixture of sulphur, coal dust and foul fumes from the oil lamp above', and claimed by the time he reached his destination he was 'near dead of asphyxiation and heat'. Blumenfeld summed up his experience thus: 'I should think these Underground railways must soon be discontinued, for they are a menace to health.'

Years later, in the 1950s, Blumenfeld's son, the future Sir John Elliot, was appointed chairman of London Transport, and was knighted for his services to the system.

> The Metropolitan Railway is, as Iago says of wine, 'a good, familiar creature, if it be well used.'
>
> *Punch*, 1868

METRO-LAND

The growing Underground network offered swift travel to and from the city, allowing commuters to settle in the calm of the suburbs.

Metro-land was a triangular area that reached from Baker Street through north-west London and out to

Buckinghamshire, Hertfordshire and Middlesex. As the Metropolitan Railway continued its expansion towards these counties, it was decided the leftover land around the tracks should be used to build new homes.

The term 'Metro-land' was coined by James Garland of the Metropolitan Railways Marketing Board in 1915, in order to get Londoners excited about country living within easy reach of the city. The idea was aimed at the lower-middle classes who could afford more spacious and comfortable accommodation out on the fringes of London. To allow for its exponential growth, it was described in promotional material as 'a country with elastic borders that each visitor can draw for himself'.

Further marketing material claimed Metro-land to be 'the most accessible and least spoiled residential district around London' with a train service 'the envy of all', adding that the climate was 'mild and equable' and the air 'clean and invigorating'.

Critics of Metro-land complained these new housing developments swallowed up nearby towns and villages, and took away their identities. However, as mortgages

became more readily available, so Metro-land's popularity grew and, startlingly, in the first 30 years of the twentieth century, villages like Pinner and Harrow Weald saw their populations soar by 800 per cent.

In 1960, Poet Laureate Sir John Betjeman wrote lovingly of the region, saying that 'Metro-land beckoned us out to lanes in beechy Bucks'.

WOMEN AND THE TUBE

The design of the earliest Tube trains, which comprised separate carriages with no adjoining doors, meant passengers' safety could be jeopardised and there were incidences of solo female travellers being sexually harassed in between stations. This led to the introduction of women-only carriages to ensure female passengers felt safe; these carriages were still in place in the 1970s on some suburban lines.

This is something that has been campaigned for again in London in recent years (but refused) and is in place on the underground railways of Delhi and Tokyo, among others. TfL takes safety very seriously and currently states on its website: 'You have the right to travel without being concerned about unwanted sexual attention of any kind,' before adding that 'leering, groping or unwanted sexual remarks' will certainly not be tolerated.

LOST PROPERTY

Since its inception in 1933, the London Underground's Lost Property Office located just by Baker Street station has seen it all. Nothing is ever thrown away, but is recycled or sold after a certain period of time, with the proceeds used to fund the office or donated to charity. It is estimated that only around 22 per cent of lost items are claimed. Umbrellas are among the most commonly lost items and the strangest things left on the Tube over the years include:

- Samurai sword
- Wedding dress
- 14-ft boat
- Box of 144 condoms
- Stuffed eagle
- Breast implants
- An occupied urn
- Park bench
- Two human skulls in a bag
- Jar of bull's sperm
- Lawnmower
- A child's slide

THE WORLD GOES UNDERGROUND

The twenty-first-century London commuter might grimace at the mention of their daily Tube journey; they might complain of the heat, overcrowding, dirt and delays; but there's no denying the inception of this transport system proved revolutionary and, once it was in use, the rest of the world pretty much followed suit.

There are close to 160 partially underground transport networks in the world, which are constantly being rebuilt and expanded. The New York City Subway boasts the most stations, with 421 sprawling over the five boroughs, while the Shanghai Metro covers the greatest distance, clocking in at 264 miles (425 km), and the Tokyo Metro claims to be the world's busiest subway system – with 3.16 billion journeys made annually. On the following pages are the top ten in terms of the number of stations they serve.

The London Underground would come between Shanghai and Beijing on this list.

1. New York City Subway, USA
Opened: 1904
No of stations: 421
Length: 209 miles (337 km)

2. Seoul Metropolitan Subway, South Korea
Opened: 1974
No of stations: 314
Length: 241.9 miles (389.3 km)

3. Paris Métro, France
Opened: 1900
No of stations: 301
Length: 134 miles (215 km)

4. Metro de Madrid, Spain
Opened: 1919
No of stations: 300
Length: 182 miles (293 km)

5. Shanghai Metro, China
Opened: 1995
No of stations: 285
Length: 264 miles (425 km)

6. Beijing Subway, China
Opened: 1969
No of stations: 218
Length: 231.2 miles (372 km)

7. Moscow Metro, Russia
Opened: 1935
No of stations: 185
Length: 190 miles (305.7 km)

8. Tokyo Metro, Japan
Opened: 1927
No of stations: 179
Length: 121.2 miles (195.1 km)

9. Mexico City Metro, Mexico
Opened: 1969
No of stations: 175
Length: 109.9 miles (176.8 km)

10. Berlin U-Bahn, Germany
Opened: 1902
No of stations: 173
Length: 91 miles (147 km)

TUBE STOP

MARYLEBONE

The area around this station takes its name from a nearby church called St Mary le Bourne, which sat on the banks of the River Tyburn, now one of London's many lost rivers. The church was named after the Virgin Mary and 'Bourne' meaning brook or river.

6

NEITHER A DRIVER NOR A PASSENGER BE

Whether you're travelling on the Tube or driving it, there are rules that need to be stuck to – official or otherwise. Passengers need to be aware of those around them, especially on a packed, hot and sticky train, and if only everyone was aware of the 'rules', a Tube carriage would be a much nicer place to be. Commuters and frequent Underground users will be aware of these already, but there might be the odd one that's slipped through the net. So pay attention! And adhere to the rules below.

UNWRITTEN RULES OF THE UNDERGROUND

🚇 **Don't make eye contact** – that's what all the free newspapers are for. The Tube isn't a particularly friendly place during rush hour, with commuters keen to simply make a quick journey and be done with it. Don't expect to make friends during peak hours; some might argue it's easier to have your face in the armpit of a stranger.

- **Don't fall asleep** – especially if you're a dribbler or liable to snore. Grab a caffeine-infused beverage and stay sharp while travelling.

- **Don't read broadsheets** – or if you do, make sure your newspaper is folded into a neat square so you don't take up the width of three seats when reading the centre spread. There's a reason why many daily papers have downsized in format in recent years – pick one of those.

- **Let passengers off the train first** – there's nothing more annoying, or in fact difficult, than having to squeeze yourself out of the mass of commuters without the added flow of extra traffic in the opposite direction.

- **If the doors are closing, let them** – Tube trains are incredibly frequent and it's likely another one will be along in two minutes. Holding or forcing doors open and potentially trapping luggage in between them will lead to delays, irritate your fellow passengers and no doubt leave you red-faced when the driver makes an announcement, citing you in particular as the reason the train has not left yet.

⊖ **Keep your feet off the seats** – and this one's official – because who knows what you've stepped in and other Tube users won't appreciate it being transferred to their clothing.

⊖ **Don't eat smelly food** – because it only reminds everyone of the confines of the Tube train. Plus you can't use the interconnecting doors when the train is moving, so once it's set off there's no escape from the stench of your egg and sardine sandwiches, or the glares from the occupants of the carriage.

⊖ **Keep your Oyster Card topped up** – the last thing you want is to be involved in a passenger pile-up at the barriers.

⊖ **Turn your iPod down** – it's unlikely the entire carriage has the same music taste as you.

⊖ **Keep to the right** – not a political persuasion, but a physical one. When passengers are in a rush, making a dash up the escalators is made all the more difficult by suitcases and stragglers blocking their swift exit.

THE PASSENGERS' TUBE

At midnight on 1 June 2008, a ban on carrying 'open containers of alcohol' was implemented across the entire London Underground, as well as the DLR and buses and trams throughout the capital. To commiserate with one another, the general public organised one last hurrah and, several hours before the ban came into effect, thousands of Londoners gathered on trains and platforms to enjoy a drink on the Underground one last time. The Circle line seemed the obvious choice for the party train and was dubbed 'Last Orders on the Underground'. Matt Wynn told the BBC he was drinking Champagne to 'show that you can drink responsibly on the Tube and not cause trouble'; however, Peter Moore said he had downed a can of beer in ten seconds and planned to ride the Circle line 'round and round until I vomit'. So drinkers were out in force. Six stations had to close to ease overcrowding and 17 people were arrested. Just your average Saturday night in London, then...

X-Factor winner Alexandra Burke filmed her video for 'Let it Go' on a Victoria-line train in April 2012 – enticing her fellow passengers, Pied Piper-style, to join her in raising the roof of the Tube carriage. A veritable disco ensues, but there isn't a drop of booze in sight.

The London Assembly's Transport Committee published a report in 2009 entitled *Too Close for Comfort: passengers' experiences of the London Underground.* The study found that more than 50 per cent of commuters claimed they were unable to board the first train at rush hour; many had to prepare themselves mentally for 'the struggle to clamber on board'; and some found they acted uncharacteristically on journeys, with one participant admitting 'I'm a different animal on the Tube to normal life. I'm a bit less interested in others.' Many passengers even said they would travel a few stops in the opposite direction in order to catch a train back that was likely to be less crowded.

In his 2012 re-election campaign, London Mayor Boris Johnson outlined his plan to take away free travel from any under-16s who refused to give up their seat for someone elderly, pregnant or disabled. Transport for London has a Young Persons' Behavioural Code in place, which advises those between the ages of 11 and 18 to act appropriately on public transport or risk having privileges withdrawn. The Code asks young people to:

⊖ Act safely

⊖ Cooperate with our staff and treat them and other passengers with respect

⊖ Use language that does not cause offence to others

⊖ Ensure you are the only person that can hear your music

⊖ Ensure you pick up all your litter

⊖ Keep your feet off seats

⊖ Give up your seat for others

GUESS THE TUBE STATION

Take a look at the rather nonsensical anagrams below and see if you can spot the jumbled stations. You'll find the answers at the end of the chapter.

A truncated moth root
Pawnbroker's ute
Eighteen knights snort
Treacle esquires
Total lightening
Streaker bet
I eternal punk
Nettle no soy
Athlete a month
A netted canal helps

TUBE-RELATED APPS

Tube users, grab your smartphones and get downloading! There's a wealth of incredibly useful London Underground-related apps out there for your browsing pleasure. Whether out and about in the capital in need of a little travel advice or planning a trip to the big smoke, there's something here for everyone – even the seasoned commuter. The below apps are, at the time of writing, either free or very reasonably priced.

- **Tube Exits** – find out which carriage to board to be closest to an exit and find the shortest transfers between lines.

- **Real London Tube** – offers the Tube map to scale with a Google Maps backdrop for a realistic view of the network and distances between stations.

- **Tube Map** – everything you could possibly need for Tube travel, with a route planner, maps, notifications and status updates.

⊖ **Nearest Tube** – find out the distance to the nearest station via your phone's camera.

⊖ **iRefund, Tube Refunds!** – a hassle-free way of claiming refunds for delayed journeys.

⊖ **Last Tube** – does what it says on the tin: type in a station and find out when the last Tube leaves.

⊖ **Tube Alarm** – be merrily woken each morning by an alarm alerting you to any problems on the line you might need that morning.

⊖ **Walk the Tube** and **Tubewalker** – because sometimes you might prefer to walk; it's good for your health and for getting to know the streets of London. Here you will find maps detailing walking routes between Tube stops – as long or as short as you like.

THE DRIVER'S SIDE OF THINGS

Line served: Piccadilly

Time as a driver: Five years

How long did it take you to train? It took me six months to fully train as a Tube driver. Training consisted of three weeks of classroom theory and three weeks of stock training, in which we learnt about our train types, how they operate, and how to deal with defects. The rest is spent out driving with an instructor until we take a 'road test' to get our licence. It doesn't take as long for trainees now.

Best part of the job: I'm left alone to do my job. I just do my allotted driving and go home. I also enjoy the flexibility of the working hours so I don't have to compromise my social life.

Worst part of the job: The monotony of driving up and down the same line, and not seeing a lot of daylight.

Memorable experiences: Someone fell unconscious on my train, so I had to do a bit of first aid and wait for the emergency services. That was quite stressful! I also had to deal with a passenger emergency alarm on my first day out alone, which freaked me out a bit.

Ever taken part in industrial action? I participated in a one-day strike in protest over job cuts on stations. I'm a member of RMT and, while I don't always agree with their reasons for striking, I do believe in supporting the union.

Experience of TfL: They are a great employer – great pay, excellent holidays and health benefits.

THE THINGS TUBE DRIVERS SAY...

Everyone's stifled the odd giggle at an out-of-the-ordinary announcement on the Underground.

⊖ 'We are delayed at this station because someone left their baby on the train at London Bridge.'

⊖ 'This is Camden Town, hold on to your purses...'

⊖ 'Like many a promising football career, this train terminates at West Ham.'

⊖ 'You are on the Underground, overground, Wombling free District line to Wimbledon.'

⊖ 'This is Knightsbridge – change here for Mr Fayed's corner shop.'

⊖ 'Step out of the way of the doors or you WILL be crushed.'

⊖ 'Quick joke: two cannibals are eating a clown. One turns to the other and says, "Does this taste funny to you?"'

⊖ 'Wakey, wakey, rise and shine! This is the end of the Jubilee line!'

⊖ 'Sorry for all the delays, there seem to be a lot of trains about this morning.'

⊖ 'This is an announcement for the blonde woman with the pram who just got on the fourth carriage. It's one thing to put your own safety at risk, quite another to ram your baby in between the doors as they are closing. In fact, it calls into question your fitness to be a parent.'

ANAGRAM ANSWERS

⊖ Tottenham Court Road

⊖ Westbourne Park

⊖ High Street Kensington

⊖ Leicester Square

⊖ Notting Hill Gate

⊖ Baker Street

⊖ Turnpike Lane

⊖ Leytonstone

⊖ Tottenham Hale

⊖ Elephant and Castle

TUBE STOP

WHITE CITY

In the early 1900s, the area around White City station was developed for the Franco-British Exhibition held in 1908. Twenty palaces and 120 exhibition buildings were constructed for the event – all whitewashed to hide the steel and concrete, hence the name. The site was also used for the Olympic Games held the same year.

7

WAR-TORN LONDON

The Underground played a pivotal role during World War One and World War Two, when thousands of Londoners sought refuge in the deep-level stations during air raids. Train services were forced to cease on certain lines to make way for those seeking shelter and people often queued all day, eager to secure a safe spot for the night on the platform below.

During World War One, the first bombs fell on London on 31 May 1915 and passenger numbers began to increase on the network as many took to riding around on trains or sitting on station platforms during air raids. It was then that the Underground Company began to encourage the public to head below ground for safety. One poster said: 'It is bomb proof down below. Underground for safety; plenty of bright trains; business as usual.'

It was a different story at the start of World War Two, however, as the use of the Underground for shelter was actively discouraged, amid fears that unsanitary conditions could spread disease and people might simply refuse to return to the surface. In 1940 notices stated that only passengers would be admitted to stations during air raids, so members of the public would naturally purchase the cheapest ticket possible and head below ground.

Later that year Londoners were openly invited to take shelter in the deep-level stations, as long as it did 'not interfere with the transport of London's workers'. As war raged on above, stations became better equipped to house the public, with 79 installing bunk beds (which slept a total of 22,000 people), first-aid posts, toilet facilities, canteens and even small libraries – and theatre groups and musicians took to providing entertainment. People generally felt safer below ground, despite several stations falling foul of bombings throughout the Blitz.

BOMBS OVER LONDON

Bombing during World War Two caused damage on the Tube network, tragically costing many lives.

- On 16 September 1940, a night raid on the city caused extensive damage to Oxford Street and 20 people were killed when a high-explosive bomb ripped through the roof of **Marble Arch** station and exploded in the tunnel. The blast travelled down past the platforms, ripping ceramic tiles from the station walls, its effect magnified due to the enclosed space.

- **Trafalgar Square** station (now part of Charing Cross) suffered at the hands of the Luftwaffe on 12 October 1940 when a bomb hit the road, exploding above the ticket hall and causing the roof to collapse. Seven people died and more than 40 were injured. During this raid, the nearby National Gallery was hit by a high-explosive bomb which dropped directly on the room that had housed many Raphael paintings prior to the war – but these were elsewhere at the time (see box below).

- The following night, a single bomb was dropped on houses near to **Bounds Green** station. The destruction of the buildings caused the collapse of one of the station tunnels, where many had taken shelter for the night. Seventeen people below ground were killed in the incident and around 20 people were injured.

⊖ Just one day later, on 14 October 1940, a bomb hit the road above **Balham** station, which was being used as an air-raid shelter, leaving a huge crater in the road into which a bus fell. The bomb caused the collapse of one of the tunnels below and burst a water main, which flooded the station. More than 60 people were killed and 70 injured.

⊖ On 11 January 1941, **Bank** station was hit, when a bomb dropped on the ticket hall, bounced down the stairs and exploded on the platform. The blast travelled down tunnels where people were sleeping and 111 people were killed, both below and above ground.

⊖ The worst civilian disaster of World War Two occurred during an air raid on 3 January 1943, when 173 people were crushed to death at **Bethnal Green** station while making their way down to the platforms below. Upon hearing a loud explosion, many people panicked and tried to push their way into the station; someone tripped at the bottom of the stairs, causing a pile-up of 300 people, mainly women and children. The incident was reported but the location was not given and its true magnitude kept under wraps. It was not until two years later that a full report on the tragedy was released.

GUARDING TREASURES

Aldwych station on the Strand was not only used extensively as an air-raid shelter during World War Two, but it played an important role in safeguarding London's art treasures. With only one platform in operation at Aldwych, the disused eastern platform was ideal for art storage, and the V&A, British Museum and National Gallery all made use of the space. The British Museum entrusted Aldwych with the safe keeping of the Elgin Marbles and the National Gallery stored some 300 paintings.

WAR SECRETS BELOW GROUND

A subterranean railway network provided London with myriad solutions during wartime. Beyond the air-raid shelters and the invaluable treasures protected by the tunnels, the government found further reasons to head underground.

Between Hyde Park Corner and Green Park on the Piccadilly line lay seldom-used Down Street station, which, having closed in 1932, provided deep-level shelter for the Emergency Railway Committee during World War Two. Winston Churchill also used the shelter as a secret base in which to hold occasional Cabinet meetings and referred to Down Street as 'the Burrow', claiming it was the only place in London he

could get a good night's sleep, far away from the sound of bombs overhead.

After the onset of war halted the extension of the Central line, a very different use was found for the stretch of tunnel running between Leytonstone and Gants Hill. Plessey had been running a munitions factory nearby, but after this was bombed in 1940, the electronics and defence firm convinced London Transport to allow it to continue operations in the tunnels. The factory location was kept well under wraps and access was via the unfinished Tube stations of Wanstead, Redbridge and Gants Hill. More than 4,000 people, mainly women, worked there over the course of four years, assembling wiring sets and telecommunications equipment, as well as producing shell fuses and cartridge cases.

WOMEN AND THE UNDERGROUND

As the majority of men headed to the front line, the women of London were tasked with keeping the city's transport system running and, during World War One, were employed on the Underground for the first time – often receiving the same wages as men. Maida Vale on the Bakerloo line was the first women-only staffed station and posters adorned the Underground, shouting about the great job the fairer sex was doing:

'Speeding millions to and from their war jobs is the wartime task of London Transport workers – 24 hours a day. It's a big job and with 18,000 of the staff in the HM Forces, it's not an easy one. London Transport is proud of the fine work of its staff – including the 11,000 women now doing such a fine job filling the ranks. Aided by many little acts of consideration on the part of passengers, the staff manage, even in these testing times, to keep the wheels running smoothly.'

DOCUMENTING THE WAR

Many artists documented the sights of World War Two in London through their work.

Official war artist Henry Moore was fascinated by the use of the stations as air-raid shelters, noting 'groups of strangers formed together in intimate groups and children asleep within feet of the passing trains'. He refused to sketch the Londoners while they slept, however, admitting 'it would have been like drawing in the hold of a slave ship'. Instead, he observed and took notes to refer to when completing his sketches elsewhere and compiled *A Shelter Sketchbook* from drawings created during 1940 and 1941.

Edward Ardizzone, another official war artist, was commissioned by National Gallery director Kenneth Clark (later Lord Clark) to paint scenes from the shelters. The resulting paintings were deemed too depressing and Ardizzone was assigned to the East End of London to document 'some places where it is known that lively scenes are taking place'.

German-born photographer Bill Brandt settled in London prior to World War Two and was commissioned by the government to photograph the public as they huddled together in Tube stations during air raids. Having previously focused on documenting the class divide in Britain, Brandt used his insights to produce moving depictions of various different Londoners faced with war.

TUBE STOP

GUNNERSBURY

Legend has it the area around this station takes its name from Gunnhildr, the niece of medieval monarch King Cnut, who lived in what we now know as Gunnersbury Park in the early eleventh century, until she was banished from England in 1044.

8

TRIUMPHS AND DISASTERS

TRIUMPHS

THE TUBE CHALLENGE

Since the 1960s, many an Underground fanatic has attempted the Tube Challenge – the feat of visiting every station on the network in the shortest time possible. You might think this one's a bit on the easy side when it comes to breaking an officially recognised World Record – after all, you spend the best part of a day sitting down. But the reality is far from it.

The official Guinness World Records rules state that an independent witness must start the master stopwatch and ceremoniously stop it at the end of the challenge. Every station on the London Underground must be visited and stations that have the same name but are geographically separate must be travelled through. Transfers between stations (e.g. when changing lines) must be completed via scheduled public transport; travel via taxi, bicycle or skateboard is not permitted;

and a log detailing the time each station is reached must be recorded. The Tube Challenge is a serious business.

The current record (set on 27 May 2011 and held by Andy James and Steve Wilson) stands at 16 hours, 29 minutes and 13 seconds.

THERE'S A FIRST TIME FOR EVERYTHING...

⊖ In 1924 the first baby to be born on the London Underground entered the world via a Bakerloo line train at Elephant & Castle. Rumours at the time suggested the baby girl had been named Thelma Ursula Beatrice Eleanor (see what they did with the initials there?), but sadly this proved untrue and it was later discovered she was in fact named Marie Cordery – and when she grew up she didn't like the Tube at all.

⊖ On 19 December 2008 Julita Kowalska gave birth to baby Jennifer at Kingsbury station on the Jubilee line; and in 2009 the first boy to start life on the Underground was born to Michelle Jenkins at London Bridge.

⊖ In November 2011, Adam King proposed to Lucy Rogers on a London Overground service, with the help a singing 'flash mob' comprised of members of his choir. Singers dotted around the carriage joined in one by one to perform a rendition of Bill Withers' 'Lovely Day', which culminated in King's successful proposal.

DID YOU KNOW...?

Former Prime Minister William Gladstone's coffin was transported to his state funeral at Westminster Abbey via the Underground in 1898. The Prince of Wales and Duke of York (who would later become Edward VII and George V respectively) were his pall-bearers. The only other coffin to travel to its funeral on the Tube belonged to philanthropist Thomas Barnardo, founder of the Barnardo's homes for disadvantaged children, and made its journey in 1905 from Liverpool Street to Barkingside.

OLYMPIC SPIRIT

On 24 July 2012, the Olympic torch travelled on the District line from Wimbledon to Wimbledon Park. Signalman John Light accompanied the torch on its Tube journey aboard a train decorated with Olympic rings. Olympics mania spilled over into the London Underground during the summer of 2012, with many an information display delivering news of medals won by Team GB and Paralympics GB, and drivers making victorious announcements for the benefit of the passengers who had peeled themselves away from their TV screens.

RECOGNISING QUALITY

Transport for London and the London Underground have been much decorated in recent years, receiving awards and accolades for various achievements. TfL was the first transport authority to receive a five-star equality rating. LU received a prestigious health award from the BBC for the way in which it deals with stress levels among staff, as well as scooping Train Operator of the Year at the Rail Business Awards and Public Transport Operator of the Year at the 'transport Oscars'. Over the years many employees have been recognised for their loyal service to the network and staff bravery is regularly noted.

DID YOU KNOW...?

Baroness Orczy supposedly conceived the idea for *The Scarlet Pimpernel* while in the booking hall at Tower Hill station.

DISASTERS

The London Underground may have revolutionised the capital's transport system and shaped the city we know today, but its story can't be told without mention of the tragedies also. We've seen how many Londoners sheltering from air raids during World War Two were victims of bombing brutality, but there have also been crashes, derailments, fires and terrorist attacks. The network learns lessons from such tragic events and uses the experiences to do its best to prevent them from happening again.

Date: 28 February 1975

Where: Moorgate

What happened: The 8.37 a.m. Northern line commuter train from Drayton Park to Moorgate didn't stop at the station as planned, but instead overshot the platform and crashed into the end of a tunnel, crushing three carriages into a space where just one would fit. The final death toll was 43, including driver Leslie Newson, despite rescue teams having worked tirelessly to free survivors from the crushed carriages. Twelve hours after the crash, 19-year-old police officer Margaret Liles was rescued from the front carriage after her foot was amputated – rescuers later spoke of her 'raw courage'. The rescue operation continued for six days, involving 1,300 firefighters, 240 police, 80 ambulance staff and 16 physicians, not to mention hospital staff and volunteers. The cause of the crash still remains something of a mystery – the driver had been in good health, as had the train, track and signalling equipment. However, the Moorgate disaster remains London's worst train crash.

What changed: As Moorgate was the terminus of a 2.5 mile arm to Drayton Park, changes were implemented across the board relating to end-of-the-line services. The signalling system was adjusted so that only a fixed 'stop' light would show on approach to a dead end, and an automatic warning system was put in place. This system would sound a horn and apply the brakes automatically should the train not slow down.

Date: 18 February 1991

Where: Victoria

What happened: A bomb had exploded under hoardings at Paddington station at 4.20 a.m., causing roof damage but no casualties. At 7 a.m. London Transport reportedly received a phone call from a man who warned: 'We are the Irish Republican Army; bombs to go off at all mainline stations in 45 minutes.' Forty minutes later, a bomb exploded in a litter bin on the main concourse at Victoria station, killing one man and injuring 38 others.

What changed: This incident, and similar such bombings that had preceded it, led to the removal of rubbish bins from all Underground and central London stations. Lockers and left-luggage storage facilities were also removed. Rubbish bins only began to reappear on the network in 2011 as part of Mayor Boris Johnson's Capital Clean-up operation to get the city shipshape before the London 2012 Olympics.

ACTS OF BRAVERY

Date: 23 November 1984

Where: Oxford Circus

What happened: At around 10.30 p.m. a fire broke out in a tunnel connecting the Bakerloo and Victoria lines. Five Tube trains – packed with more than a thousand passengers between them – were caught in the fray, the smoke slowly infiltrating the carriages. Off-duty police officer Peter Power was travelling on one of the trains. He retrieved his uniform from his bag, put it on and attempted to calm down the panicking passengers. Finding the guard's van, Power reassured those on board, via the PA system and a few white lies, that help was on its way, when in fact he had no idea if it was or not. After several hours, the search party arrived;

Power instructed passengers to form an orderly line and ensured everyone exited the train swiftly and sensibly. 14 people were treated in hospital for smoke inhalation, among them nine members of Underground staff and one police officer, who had scoured the smoke-filled platforms for any lingering passengers. The enquiry that followed stated the cause was likely to have been a lit cigarette end, which had found its way into a tunnel containing building materials and subsequently set them alight.

What changed: Smoking had been banned on all Underground trains since July 1984, but the Oxford Circus fire led to an extension of the ban to cover all sub-surface stations.

Date: 18 November 1987

Where: King's Cross

What happened: A small fire, believed to have started when a discarded match was dropped into some litter beneath a wooden escalator, grew into a blazing inferno within only a few minutes. A smoking ban in stations had been brought in after the Oxford Circus fire, but passengers often lit cigarettes as they were travelling up the escalators towards the exit.

The slope of the escalator transporting the flames caused what is known as the 'trench effect' – whereby hot gases from the flames clung to the stairs, thus preheating the material ahead, releasing flammable gasses from the wood and causing the fire to spread rapidly. This resulted in a fireball sweeping up the escalator, engulfing the ticket hall, producing plumes of thick, black smoke and plunging the station into darkness. In all, 31 people were killed.

What changed: Tube stations were generally stripped of anything that could burn and produce fumes.

AN EYEWITNESS ACCOUNT

Date: 7 July 2005

Where: In the tunnels between Aldgate and Liverpool Street; Russell Square and King's Cross; and Edgware Road and Paddington.

What happened: During the morning rush hour, three bombs were detonated on Tube trains on the Circle and Piccadilly lines; almost an hour later another bomb exploded on a number 30 bus in Tavistock Square. London fell into a state of chaos and it was soon discovered the explosions had been the work of four suicide bombers. Fifty-two people died as a result and 700 were injured.

Twenty-three-year-old Caroline Steele was on the Piccadilly line train heading to Russell Square, sat just 2–3 m from where the bomb was detonated. 'I was on the end of a row of seats with a glass panel to my left and the bomber was stood in the space by the double doors just next to me,' she says. 'About 30 seconds after we left King's Cross, I wasn't aware of a noise, just a massive force coming from my left, which knocked me over; I couldn't see anything and the train was shaking around. What sticks in my mind so clearly is when you're on a Tube train everything is so clean and bright, but all the lights had gone so there was this dull, orange emergency light and all the poles were blasted out of position at weird angles.' Caroline managed to make her way off the train via the driver's cab and walked down the tracks to Russell Square station.

Her injuries were relatively superficial considering her proximity to the explosion. 'I had about 30 stitches in my head and face, and the entire left-hand side of my body was bruised a greenish-purple colour for quite a while,' she says. 'I had an interview with the police and they said I was the luckiest person they'd spoken to considering how close I was – and 26 people died on that train. One metre in another direction and things could've been very different.'

Ten months passed before Caroline felt comfortable travelling on the Tube and slowly but surely she began to feel more positive. 'It's an incredibly horrible thing to have happened, whether or not I was a part of it, but I'm grateful for how lucky I was. I'm also really proud of myself for overcoming my fear of the Tube and now I use it every day.'

What changed: Press coverage of the inquests into the events of 7 July 2005 criticised the speed at which emergency services responded to the incidents, further hindered by a communication breakdown due to certain mobile networks reaching capacity. Much changed in the years that followed as the events of the day were scrutinised, and London Underground and London Ambulance Service have since introduced more efficient communication systems.

TUBE STOP

MILE END

This station originally took its name from the milestone marking its position 1 mile east of the gates of London. Pedants will note, however, that Stepney Green was in fact more accurately placed to receive the name, but the growing settlement at Mile End needed a name.

9

THE TUBE AND THE ARTS

Whether you spy it in a James Bond film, a music video or a TV series centred around its very existence, the London Underground is always appearing in popular culture. Naturally so, as it is integral to the capital and at the heart of its structure – some might even argue that the Tube *is* London. And there's no getting away from the fact that authors, screenwriters and poets have drawn on the network to inspire whole projects, spawned from a love of or deep fascination with the system. The influence of the Underground has trickled into the nation's consciousness and spurred a wealth of creativity over its 150-plus years.

ON THE BIG SCREEN

Adding a touch of reality to offset big-screen glamour, Underground references in London-based films generally build a sure sense of monotony around a character's daily grind (e.g. *Bridget Jones's Diary* and *Bridget Jones: The Edge of Reason*); but then there's tragedy, too (e.g. *Atonement*). The network has also been known to set the scene for grisly horror films, where, trapped in the dark underground, no one can hear you scream…

Take 1972 cult British horror *Death Line*, which spins us a disturbing yarn involving a cannibalistic killer – descended from railway workers trapped in a tunnel and simply forgotten about – living on the Underground near Russell Square. Or 2004's *Creep*,

which finds the film's heroine stuck beneath the city surface after hours with, wait for it, another insane cannibal. Along similarly sinister lines came Danny Boyle's *28 Days Later* and the breakdown of life as we know it as the majority of the population becomes infected with 'rage', zombie-style: watch out for both Bank and Canary Wharf stations in this one, along with some DLR train footage for good measure.

So, it would seem London's subterranean transport system and its dank network of tunnels is rather fitting for the darker side of cinema. And we mustn't forget 1981's *An American Werewolf in London* and a particularly hairy (pun intended) chase scene through a Northern line pedestrian tunnel at Tottenham Court Road station.

Then, of course, there's the rather more middle-of-the-road *Sliding Doors* – a dual-aspect analysis of how Gwyneth Paltrow's life pans out depending on whether she catches a certain Tube or not. London transport pedants have noted that despite signage to the contrary, the station is actually Waterloo, which means the train in question is a Waterloo & City line train bound for the depot. The station sign in the film says Embankment, but the Waterloo & City line only runs between two stations – Waterloo and Bank...

Three and Out sees Mackenzie Crook assume the role of a Tube driver who unfortunately witnesses two 'one unders' in the space of a month. With the word on the Underground that three in a month spells retirement on a decade's full pay, he sets about finding a willing candidate. No spoilers here!

Everyone's favourite double-O makes several visits to the fictional disused Tube station Vauxhall Cross in *Die Another Day*, which is being used as a secret base for M and Q et al. In the guise of Bond, Pierce Brosnan is presented with a stealth Aston Martin, which emerges from one of the tunnels. Despite looking remarkably realistic, apparently this was just a set somewhere, inspired by Aldwych station.

BEAMED INTO A HOME NEAR YOU

It's funny how we're so accepting of the fictional Tube stations dreamt up for long-running TV series. 'Of course Walford East is a real station,' we cry, reaching for a Tube map, certain it must be on there. 'It's in Albert Square, for God's sake!' forgetting, momentarily, in a soap-induced blur, that Albert Square doesn't actually exist either – except on a closed set in Elstree Studios in Hertfordshire (see Chapter 10 for more on the EastEnders' Underground connection). The same could be said for the UK's much-loved emergency services dramas *The Bill* and *London's Burning*, with their Sun Hill and Blackwall Tube stations respectively. The names sound perfectly acceptable, as if they should exist as Underground stations – in fact, why don't they?

Doctor Who scriptwriters have always had a penchant for sending their protagonist into London's transport Underworld; from William Hartnell taking residence in a disused Underground station, the fictional World's End, in the 1960s; to Christopher Eccleston and Billie Piper's first encounter in the Queen's Arcade shopping centre featuring a Tube station of the same name.

Then there's Neil Gaiman and Lenny Henry's *Neverwhere*, which aired in the 1990s and is centred around the Underground – or 'London Below', a rather more sinister alternate reality to 'London above'. Many of the below-ground scenes were filmed in disused deep-level stations, the Tube map features heavily and various characters' monikers are derived from station names – such as Serpentine of the Seven Sisters, an angel called Islington and a load of monks referred to as the Black Friars.

Fans of the Underground will love *Tube Tales*, a selection of nine short films from 1999 featuring many a familiar face, with the likes of Ray Winstone, Dexter Fletcher, Kelly Macdonald, Denise van Outen and Rachel Weisz to name a few. Almost entirely shot on the Underground, the films were based on experiences submitted by passengers to *Time Out* magazine and cover everything from birds and preachers on trains to drug running, suicide, lost children and ghosts.

ON LOCATION

The Tube has merrily featured in many a beloved TV series and Hollywood blockbuster, but where were they actually filmed? Well, as it's a disused station that has been well kept and restored, Aldwych has been a popular choice more recently. The likes of *Atonement, The Edge of Love, V for Vendetta, Primeval, Creep* and countless others were all filmed down there. The once disused platform at Charing Cross (now in service as part of the Jubilee line) was also used for various filming projects, with the film crews of *Spooks* and *28 Weeks Later* heading below ground there; *Neverwhere* was filmed at the disused Down Street; and the original Wood Lane station, which stopped serving the public in 1947, was the location of choice for several *Doctor Who* episodes in the 1960s, as well as 1970s kids' sci-fi series *The Tomorrow People*.

FROM THE PLATFORM TO THE PAGE

Many works of literature feature the Tube as a central character in the story, integral to the plot and character development: there's Julian Barnes' *Metroland*, with the Metropolitan line featuring heavily, as well as displaying contempt for Metro-land itself; Keith Lowe's *Tunnel Visions*, where the protagonist is challenged to visit every station on the network in a day; and Barbara Vine (aka Ruth Rendell)'s *King Solomon's Carpet*, where King Solomon's Carpet is actually a metaphor for the London Underground.

Long before these, in *The Three Clerks* published in 1857, Anthony Trollope comments on the growth of

London, brought on by the formation of the railways: 'It is very difficult nowadays to say where the suburbs of London come to an end and where the country begins. The railways have turned the countryside into a city.'

While in Aldous Huxley's *Crome Yellow*, cynical philosopher Mr Scogan finds solace underground, away from the outside world: 'Travel by Tube and you see nothing but the works of man,' he says, noting the fine construction of the network and controversially declaring 'preserve me from nature'.

And who could forget the Lost and Found? There was Michael Bond's Paddington Bear, the marmalade addict who was discovered at Paddington station by the Brown family; and Jack Worthing of Oscar Wilde's *The Importance of Being Earnest*, potentially doomed to lose the love of his life due to having been discovered, as a baby, in a handbag in a cloakroom at Victoria station – 'a HANDBAG?'

Although Hogwarts is sadly inaccessible by Tube, there is, of course, Platform 9¾ at King's Cross station. Albus Dumbledore, everyone's favourite wizardly headmaster, refuses to repair Harry Potter's lightning-shaped scar, explaining how useful scars can be: 'I have one myself above my left knee which is a perfect map of the London Underground.'

WALKING THE TUBE

In a bid to discover every nook and cranny of the capital, Mark Mason set about walking the entire length of the network and documented it in his book *Walk the Lines: The London Underground, Overground*. A fascinating insight into the city by way of its underground transport system, but from the surface, Mason's account of his travels offers trivia of the highest order, a wealth of interesting history and a glimpse of how much one can miss when staying below ground.

As we came up Baker Street,
Where tubes and trains and 'buses meet
There's a touch of fog and a touch of sleet;
And we go on up Hampstead way
Towards the closing of the day...
But here we are in the Finchley Road
With a drizzling rain and a skidding 'bus
And the twilight settling down on us.

'Finchley Road' – Ford Madox Hueffer, 1916

ALL IN THE GAME

With Lara Croft finding herself in the disused Aldwych station (albeit with larger platforms and many more tunnels than the original) in a level of *Tomb Raider 3*, and *Call of Duty: Modern Warfare 3* featuring a train hijack from Canary Wharf to Westminster, the Underground doesn't escape the world of video games either.

THE TUBE GOES POP

The video for The Prodigy's 1996 number one 'Firestarter' was filmed in a disused tunnel next to Aldwych station. The video aired on *Top of the Pops* and received a record number of complaints, as many viewers claimed that it fixated on arson and that frontman Keith Flint scared their children. Other artists to film music videos almost exclusively on the Tube include Suede ('Saturday Night'), Feeder ('Suffocate') and Alexandra Burke ('Let it Go'). For some vintage footage, see Soft Cell's 'Bedsitter' and 'Do it Again' by the Kinks.

BUSKING ON THE TUBE

Love them or hate them, the Tube wouldn't be the same without its buskers. The music echoing through the winding tunnels adds a certain *je ne sais quoi* to the Underground experience, dare I say it, lifting one's spirits when powering through the endless passages on a daily basis. The practice is widely policed in Underground stations, with only licensed buskers allowed in designated spots. There are 39 pitches across 25 central London stations, recognised by a semicircular floor graphic, which LU refers to as a 'mini-stage'. Potential buskers must impress a panel of LU staff, industry experts and talent scouts to scoop one of the coveted licences. Busking was considered a nuisance and banned on the Underground throughout the twentieth century, until the licensed scheme was implemented in 2003 and cellist Julian Lloyd-Webber became its first official busker – for one day only and for charity.

TUBE STOP

CHALK FARM

This station's name is derived from a seventeenth-century farmstead known as Lower Chalcot Farm, which was located in the area. The farm lay in Chalcot Manor and became a popular tavern in the eighteenth century, before the area was redeveloped in the late nineteenth century to provide much-needed housing.

10

ABANDONED STATIONS

London may have been amazingly forward-thinking in introducing the first underground railway to the world but, as with all ambitious projects, there was plenty of room for error. Especially during the 1930s, many deep-level Tube stations were closed or relocated due to lack of use and funds to keep them in service. The remains of the so-called ghost stations can be spotted on street corners and from train windows in the shadows between stations.

Tours of abandoned stations are now rare, as health and safety issues come into play, but this could be set to change. Entrepreneur Ajit Chambers waved goodbye to a life in the banking sector to set up the Old London Underground Company, with the hope of putting the 26 abandoned stations in the capital to good use – by adapting the platform spaces and tunnels to offer Blitz-themed tourist experiences, art galleries, nightclubs and sports facilities, among other things. 'Essentially I've found a huge product and an ability to bring money into the country,' he asserts.

Chambers is working with investors and the Mayor of London to reopen the disused stations, with Brompton Road the first in their sights. Plans for this station include a roof garden, a meeting space in the old war rooms (used by Churchill and his cabinet during World War Two) and a climbing wall in one of the deep-level shafts. With a bit of innovative thinking – for example, spraying transparent rubber over original platform tiling to protect against wear and tear – Chambers hopes to refurbish many of the stations' features to their former glory.

'Stripping them out is not the point,' he says, 'but making every view of the history, lit properly and with a bit of atmosphere in there, is what we're looking for.'

HUNTING FOR FORGOTTEN STATIONS

Being whisked across the capital on a tubular train is such a regular occurrence for most Londoners that they tend to switch off once on board. But peeking out of the windows as the train speeds through darkened tunnels can reveal more than you might have thought.

Arm yourself with the necessary information, ample refreshments and a healthy imagination, and you'll be surprised at what is lurking in the depths between some of the Underground's busy stations. Bearing in mind that many of them were abandoned in the earlier half of the twentieth century is important – don't expect to see shiny ex-stations, beautifully maintained and representing a bygone era – many of these so-called ghost stations are either bricked up or used for storage purposes, but discovering their whereabouts via certain little clues can be rather satisfying, depending on your leisure preferences, of course.

ESSENTIAL TO ABANDONED-STATION SPOTTING

⊖ Do your research – Just peering out of the windows spontaneously and hoping for the best won't amount to much. In between most stations there's nothing much to see.

⊖ Store up your patience – As it all happens so quickly, you might not see anything the first time and may have to travel that stop several times. Even after a few journeys you might not see what you were hoping for, but don't despair.

⊖ Exercise your imagination – You might see a large space and a few piles of bricks, but imagine the platform that used to stand there and attempt to restore the station to its former glory in your mind's eye.

⊖ Don't be put off – It's best to either ignore your fellow passengers when concentrating on spying old stations, or invite them to join in.

⊖ Take supplies – Don't forget to pack your (neutral-smelling) sandwiches, as you might be down there for a while.

As you travel between stations, with your nose pressed against the glass and hands cupped around your eyes, it's difficult not to fall into a trance-like state, as the train rushes past miles and miles of electrical wires, their bright colours dancing on your retinas. You will find regained composure, as if with the snap of a hypnotist's fingers, brought on by the changing surfaces of the tunnel walls, a sudden doorway or widening track space.

Here are some of the highlights you might encounter on a day's adventure hunting for forgotten spots on the Underground.

- Between Hyde Park Corner and Green Park on the Piccadilly line, to your right you'll catch a glimpse of the remnants of one of **Down Street**'s platforms and the space where the tracks once were. Down Street opened in 1907 and was in use until 1932, when it was closed due to its close proximity to Dover Street station (renamed Green Park shortly after). It also played an important role during World War Two (see Chapter 7).

- Again on the Piccadilly line, heading west between Knightsbridge and South Kensington, to your right you'll spot the cast-iron tunnel cladding switch to brickwork and a blink-and-you'll-miss-it walkway through the wall. This is the site of the bricked-up **Brompton Road** station, in operation between 1906 and 1934, closed, again, due to lack of use and too little distance between Tube stops.

Travelling eastbound on the Central line between White City and Shepherd's Bush, look to your left as you enter the tunnel and you'll see it widen significantly to reveal a platform area where the old **Wood Lane** station once sat. Opened in 1908 to serve the Franco-British Exhibition and the London Olympics held in the same year, despite being viewed as a temporary measure, Wood Lane remained in use until 1947 when White City was opened nearby. The station building and depot remained until 2003 when it was demolished to

make way for the gargantuan Westfield shopping centre. A new Wood Lane station was opened in 2008, this time operating on both the Circle and Hammersmith & City lines.

Again on the Central line and the busy route from Tottenham Court Road to Holborn. Take a look to your right as you approach Holborn from the west and you'll notice the tunnel open up to reveal a small set of steps leading to the bare remains of a platform, along with bits of equipment and track paraphernalia. This once belonged to **British Museum** station, opened in 1900, but closed in 1933, owing to Holborn station lying only 100 yards away. Rumours abounded that British Museum station was haunted by an Ancient Egyptian mummy and, shortly before its closure, *The Times* offered a cash reward to anyone who would spend the night alone there. No one did.

On to the Northern line, heading north between Old Street and Angel, you'll spy the remnants of **City Road** station to both your left and right. On both sides the tunnel widens to reveal where its platforms perhaps once stood and a separate tunnel can be viewed on the right. City Road was opened in 1901 but passenger numbers started low and remained so, leading to its closure in 1922. The station was reopened during World War Two, but only for use as an air-raid shelter.

Remaining on the Northern line, heading northbound from Hampstead to Golders Green, on your right you can spot a partially built platform belonging to **North End** (often referred to as **Bull & Bush**) station, along with a small set of steps and various building materials. North End Is unique to the Tube network in that building work began around 1904 but the station never opened. Had it been a successful project, it would have been the deepest station on the network, plummeting 221 ft (67.3 m) below the surface; however, due to planning permission issues and its sparsely populated location, the work was abandoned in 1906.

SOUTH KENTISH TOWN

South Kentish Town opened on the Northern line between Camden Town and Kentish Town in 1907, but was closed in 1924 due to dwindling passenger numbers. Shortly after its closure, a train stopped at the station, held at a red signal, and a passenger mistakenly hopped off. Realising his mistake, he quickly got back on the train, but this supposedly inspired John Betjeman to write the short story *South Kentish Town,* which was broadcast on the BBC Home Service in January 1951, and tells the tale of Basil Green and how he came to end up there.

Betjeman describes passengers' annoyance at trains stopping at South Kentish Town as nobody ever wanted to get off, but says: 'It had its uses. It was a rest home for tired ticket-collectors.' He charts the demise of the Underground station and explains that, despite its closing, trains still rattled through.

Green is a creature of habit, who catches the Tube from Kentish Town to the Strand every day, counting the stops and barely looking up from his newspaper. So, when his train home unexpectedly stops at South Kentish Town, he alights from it, his eyes never leaving the *Evening Standard*. Green finds himself on a darkened platform and, despite many attempts, is unable to grasp the attention of passing train drivers. After a little exploration of the station and climbing up the lift shaft and down again, Green admits defeat for the night and curls up on the platform, using his *Evening Standard* as a pillow.

And so the story abruptly finishes and we can only wonder what became of poor Basil Green...

AN UNDERGROUND STATION ON THE THIRD FLOOR

Not really a ghost station, but interesting enough in its own right is West Ashfield, which actually sits on the third floor of an office building in West Kensington. This mocked-up station is used as a training facility for London Underground staff and is fully kitted out with all the signage you'd find in a modern Tube station: LED displays, platform markings and a small section of Tube train. Despite no trains entering or leaving this rather surreal 'station', the training experience comes complete with rumbling sound effects and fans to simulate the effect of the train's arrival.

FINE EXAMPLE

Aldwych station is a particularly special example of a disused station, as it closed relatively recently and is therefore in rather better condition than the others. Opened as Strand station in 1907, it was designed to appeal to theatregoers in the West End but, due to its placement at the end of a short branch (or twig) off the Piccadilly line, it wasn't widely used. The station was closed in 1940 for use as a full-time air-raid shelter during World War Two and reopened in 1946, but passenger numbers did not increase, leading to a restricted service from 1958 and closure in 1994.

Every now and again, Aldwych is opened up to the public and a limited number of station tours take place in association with the London Transport Museum. This provides a rare opportunity to step inside the well-kept station, peer down the darkened lift shaft, wander along the platforms, and admire the old Tube maps and posters adorning the walls.

Keep your eyes firmly on www.ltmuseum.co.uk for any future tours.

SOMEWHERE IN THE EAST END...

Arguably the most famous ghost station of them all, as it exists fictionally on the District line but physically can only be found on Elstree Studios' EastEnders set, Walford East is worthy of some recognition here. Just a hop and a skip from the infamous Albert Square, Walford East sits between Bow Road and West Ham on the District and Hammersmith & City lines (only on fictional, EastEnders-related Tube maps, of course), taking the place of Bromley-by-Bow.

The 'Enders Tube station is almost as old as the soap itself, appearing for the first time in 1985, just a few months after the programme was first broadcast on BBC1. The station has seen its fair share of drama, with many a significant arrival (Alfie Moon, Stacey Slater), departure (Zoe Slater, Little Mo, Yolande Trueman, Charlie Slater) and birth (Dawn Swann's waters broke on a District line train) in recent years.

Charlie Slater's exit via Walford East allowed viewers a first look at the platform (please contain your excitement). There was once talk of Walford West, but no one has ever glimpsed it.

TUBE STOP

MIND THE GAP

BAKER STREET

Baker Street sits on the road of the same name, which was named after William Baker, who built it in the early 1800s. The street has been immortalised in song by Gerry Rafferty and in literature by Sherlock Holmes' creator Sir Arthur Conan Doyle, with the fictional detective residing at 221b Baker Street.

11

GHOSTS OF THE TUBE

There have been countless reports of ghost sightings and unnatural phenomena on the London Underground. Whether you believe the eyewitness accounts and the stories that surround the ghostly circumstances is up to you, but they make for a good yarn – especially when told in a darkened room (or corner of a deserted, murky Tube station) with a torch held under your chin.

ALDGATE

The area in which Aldgate station sits – the East End of the City of London – has experienced its fair share of horrors over the centuries. The station building was built over one of the largest seventeenth-century plague pits in London – Aldgate suffered more than 4,000 plague deaths; Catherine Eddowes was murdered by Jack the Ripper in nearby Mitre Square in 1888;

and on 7 July 2005 one of the four bombs detonated across London exploded between Liverpool Street and Aldgate. So followers of the paranormal have noted much unusual activity at the station over the years. One night a track worker slipped and fell onto the live rail; 20,000 volts shot through his body and he was lucky to survive. When he came to, his colleagues said they had spied the ghostly figure of a woman stroking his hair just before he fell.

MOST HAUNTED

Aldwych – a ghost in itself as it closed in 1994 – has seen a hubbub of alleged ghostly activity. Well, certainly enough to attract Yvette Fielding and crew to film an episode of *Most Haunted* in the tunnels in 2002. Aldwych occupies a spot on the Strand where the Royal Strand Theatre once stood, before its demolition in 1905 to make way for the Piccadilly line station. It is believed a certain actress haunts the station – one whose career was cut short by the theatre's closure – and many fluffers have reported visions of a shadowy figure on the tracks as they cleaned the rails late at night. *Most Haunted*'s team of paranormal experts wandered the tunnels, noting questionable shadowy figures, the presence of three spirits and the appearance of orb-like lights on photographs.

BANK

Located in the heart of the City, Bank station opened in 1900 within close proximity of the Bank of England and is said to reek of the paranormal. This deep-level station is supposedly haunted by a woman whose brother, Philip Whitehead, worked as a cashier at the Bank of England. After Whitehead was executed in 1811 for forgery, his sister Sarah – unable to accept he was gone – continued to wait outside the bank every evening for him to finish work. She did this for 40 years until she died and it is believed she continues her search for him down on the platforms of Bank station. Her mourning dress has led to her ghost being dubbed the 'Black Nun'.

DID YOU KNOW…?

Legend has it that the grave of warrior queen Boadicea lies under Platform 10 at King's Cross station.

BETHNAL GREEN

As the site of the worst civilian disaster of World War Two (see chapter 7), Bethnal Green figures highly in the paranormal stakes. The tragic events of 3 March 1943 saw 173 lives lost – mainly women and children – and a memorial plaque has been placed at the station in remembrance. Over the years station staff have reported the sounds of children crying and women screaming for extended periods of time.

> The forthcoming end of the world will be hastened by the construction of the railways burrowing into infernal regions and thereby disturbing the Devil.
>
> Rev Dr John Cumming, 1860

COVENT GARDEN

Many of the ghost stories associated with the Tube involve protagonists who existed before the station or even the network was built. In this instance, Covent Garden station was erected on the site of a bakery, which the ghost in question already frequented. Said ghost, William Terriss, was once a popular actor treading the boards at the neighbouring Adelphi Theatre when he was murdered as he approached the stage door one night. Terriss had been providing struggling actor Richard Prince with financial aid but, when the money stopped in December 1897, Prince waited for Terriss at his private entrance to the theatre and stabbed him to death. Reports have been made of sightings of a tall, ghostly gentleman in Victorian dress and white gloves, as well as knocking sounds, and light switches flicking on and off. A plaque can be seen near the stage door of the Adelphi, citing Terriss as 'Hero of the Adelphi melodramas'.

TUBE STOP

MIND THE GAP

WHITECHAPEL

This east London station takes its name from
the whitewashed church of St Mary Matfelon,
which was originally built in the 1300s and,
as a well-known local landmark, was often
referred to as 'the white chapel'. The church
was destroyed by fire on several occasions
and dutifully rebuilt each time, until it was
decimated in World War Two and its ruins
removed to make way for St Mary's Park,
now known as Altab Ali Park.

12

THE FUTURE

Every Tube commuter will have experienced the overcrowding of the system. They will have felt their heart sink as they approach a central London station come 5 p.m., only to be greeted with the all-too-familiar sight of the criss-crossed metal gates drawn over the entrance. In a bid to ease rush-hour congestion and make the narrow platforms safer, this currently seems to be the only way to handle the situation.

Now carrying four million passengers daily, you could argue London has outgrown its transport network. The Victorian system was an astonishing feat, revolutionising transport and promoting the growth of the capital, but it has also proved restrictive when it comes to increasing efficiency.

As the number of people using the Tube increases year on year, more and more Londoners are relying on it to cart them from A to B. TfL has outlined an extensive and ambitious upgrade strategy to increase capacity during peak hours by as much as 65 per cent on some lines.

> The London Underground's Victorian heritage is both its charm and its burden.
>> Tim O'Toole, former managing director of
>> London Underground, 2008

MAKING IMPROVEMENTS

In more recent years we've seen changes across the network, including high-capacity signalling systems on several lines, more efficient trains in service on the Victoria and Metropolitan lines, and plans to roll out new stock across the Circle, District and Hammersmith & City lines – with a full upgrade of the sub-surface routes due to be completed in 2018. There is also talk of phasing in 'driverless' trains, as seen on the DLR.

Key interchange stations such as Victoria, Tottenham Court Road, Paddington, Bond Street and Bank are either in the process of being extended or have extension projects in the pipeline to prepare them for Crossrail (see below).

Planned works undoubtedly lead to disruption across the network but, as Mike Brown, managing director of London Underground explains: 'Without the line upgrades the infrastructure will continue to deteriorate – the Tube would gradually grind to a halt, unable to maintain current service levels or meet future demand. The line upgrades are not therefore a luxury, they are absolutely essential.'

While David Waboso, director for capital programmes and in charge of the Tube upgrade, assures London Underground users via the TfL website that 'a bit of disruption now is the price we pay for a much better Tube in the future'. He adds: 'Of course with this brand new kit there are teething troubles but we will iron them out.'

COOLING DOWN

It's estimated to be 10°C hotter on the Tube than at the surface above, and TfL has struggled for years to lower the temperature below ground, with large industrial fans in walkways at the height of summer a regular sight. But new air-conditioned trains are being introduced on subsurface lines, and works to improve ventilation and introduce air-cooling methods at deep-level stations are under way.

DID YOU KNOW?

The Tube achieved the Carbon Trust Standard in 2010 in recognition of its efforts to use energy-efficient solutions where possible. These include regenerative braking measures on new trains to recycle up to 25 per cent of energy used and working towards identifying low-carbon technologies for future design projects.

CROSSRAIL

The biggest and most imminent change to the London Underground is the introduction of Crossrail, the ambitious project currently under way to link Heathrow Airport and Berkshire with Essex via the depths of the City. The line will call at 37 stations and more than £14 billion has been procured to fund the project.

Crossrail aims to be a 'sustainable railway', transporting much of the materials used in its construction via river, introducing energy-efficient measures on trains and eventually offering a reliable service that will take cars off the road.

THE TRAINS

According to Crossrail, the proposed energy-efficient trains will be lighter than current models, stretch to 200 m in length and feature:

- Sleek, spacious, air-conditioned interiors

- A design that caters for those with restricted mobility

- Level boarding at central stations and wide gangways between carriages

- On-train systems featuring real-time travel information for those meeting connecting services

MAKING CONNECTIONS

The Underground is making a concerted effort to move with the times and provide a service that is up to date in both an engineering and a technological sense. With free Wi-Fi now available on the Underground lines, you can be connected to the world above whatever your location. Of course, opinions may be divided over the fact that you can be reached anywhere – even far below the streets of London – with some no doubt previously seeing their Tube journey as welcome respite from a barrage of emails.

The Underground is still for me the most romantic and mysterious part of London.

David Piper – *The Companion Guide to London*

APPENDIX 1: ACTIVE LONDON UNDERGROUND STATIONS

Alphabetical list, including opening dates and lines served.

Abbey Road
Line(s) served: DLR
First connected to the network: 31 August 2011

Acton Town (known as Mill Hill Park from 1879–1910)
Line(s) served: District, Piccadilly
Opened: 1 July 1879

Aldgate
Line(s) served: Circle, Metropolitan
Opened: 18 November 1876

Aldgate East
Line(s) served: District, Hammersmith & City
Opened: 6 October 1884 (relocated 31 October 1938)

All Saints
Line(s) served: DLR
Opened: 31 August 1987

Alperton (known as Perivale-Alperton from 1903–10)
Line(s) served: Piccadilly
Opened: 28 June 1903

Amersham (known as Amersham & Chesham Bois from 1922–34)
Line(s) served: Metropolitan
Opened: 1 September 1892

Angel
Line(s) served: Northern
Opened: 17 November 1901

Archway (known as Highgate from 1907–39, Archway (Highgate) from 1939–41 and Highgate (Archway) from 1941–47)
Line(s) served: Northern
Opened: 22 June 1907

Arnos Grove
Line(s) served: Piccadilly
Opened: 19 September 1932

Arsenal (known as Gillespie Road from 1906–32 and Arsenal (Highbury Hill): 1932–1960)
Line(s) served: Piccadilly
Opened: 15 December 1906

Baker Street
Line(s) served: Bakerloo, Circle, Hammersmith & City, Jubilee, Metropolitan
Opened: 10 January 1863

Balham
Line(s) served: Northern
Opened: 6 December 1926

Bank (known as City on the Waterloo & City line from 1898–1940)
Line(s) served: Central, DLR, Northern, Waterloo & City
Opened: 8 August 1898

Barbican (known as Aldersgate Street from 1865–1910, Aldersgate from 1910–23 and Aldersgate & Barbican from 1923–68)
Line(s) served: Circle, Hammersmith & City, Metropolitan
Opened: 23 December 1865

Barking
Line(s) served: District, Hammersmith & City
First connected to the network: 2 June 1902

Barkingside
Line(s) served: Central
First connected to the network: 31 May 1948

Barons Court
Line(s) served: District, Piccadilly
Opened: 9 September 1874

Bayswater (known as Bayswater (Queen's Road) & Westbourne
Grove from 1923–33, Bayswater (Queen's Road) from 1933–46
and Bayswater (Queensway) from 1946–phased out)
Line(s) served: Circle, District
Opened: 1 October 1868

Beckton
Line(s) served: DLR
Opened: 28 March 1994

Beckton Park
Line(s) served: DLR
Opened: 28 March 1994

Becontree
Line(s) served: District
First connected to the network: 18 July 1932

Belsize Park
Line(s) served: Northern
Opened: 22 June 1907

Bermondsey
Line(s) served: Jubilee
Opened: 17 September 1999

Bethnal Green
Line(s) served: Central
Opened: 4 December 1946

Blackfriars
Line(s) served: Circle, District
First connected to the network: 30 May 1870

Blackhorse Road
Line(s) served: Victoria
First connected to the network: 1 September 1968

Blackwall
Line(s) served: DLR
Opened: 28 March 1994

Bond Street
Line(s) served: Central, Jubilee
Opened: 24 September 1900

Borough
Line(s) served: Northern
Opened: 18 December 1890

Boston Manor (known as Boston Road from 1883–1911)
Line(s) served: Piccadilly
Opened: 1 May 1883

Bounds Green
Line(s) served: Piccadilly
Opened: 19 September 1932

Bow Church
Line(s) served: DLR
Opened: 31 August 1987

Bow Road
Line(s) served: District, Hammersmith & City
Opened: 11 June 1902

Brent Cross (known as Brent from 1923–76)
Line(s) served: Northern
Opened: 19 November 1923

Brixton
Line(s) served: Victoria
Opened: 23 July 1971

Bromley-by-Bow (known as Bromley from 1902–68)
Line(s) served: District, Hammersmith & City
First connected to the network: 2 June 1902

Buckhurst Hill
Line(s) served: Central
First connected to the network: 21 November 1948

Burnt Oak (known as Burnt Oak (Watling) from 1928–50)
Line(s) served: Northern
Opened: 27 October 1924

Caledonian Road
Line(s) served: Piccadilly
Opened: 15 December 1906

Camden Town
Line(s) served: Northern
Opened: 22 June 1907

Canada Water
Line(s) served: East London, Jubilee
Opened: 17 September 1999

Canary Wharf
Line(s) served: DLR, Jubilee
Opened: 31 August 1987

Canning Town
Line(s) served: DLR, Jubilee
First connected to the network: 28 March 1994

Cannon Street
Line(s) served: Circle, District
Opened: 6 October 1884

Canons Park (known as Canons Park (Edgware) from 1932–33)
Line(s) served: Jubilee
Opened: 10 December 1932

Chalfont & Latimer (known as Chalfont Road from 1889–1915)
Line(s) served: Metropolitan
Opened: 8 July 1889

Chalk Farm
Line(s) served: Northern
Opened: 22 June 1907

Chancery Lane (known as Chancery Lane (Gray's Inn): 1934–phased out)
Line(s) served: Central
Opened: 30 July 1900

Charing Cross (known as Trafalgar Square on the Bakerloo line from 1906–79 and Strand on the Northern line from 1915–79)
Line(s) served: Bakerloo, Northern
Opened: 10 March 1906

Chesham
Line(s) served: Metropolitan
Opened: 8 July 1889

Chigwell
Line(s) served: Central
First connected to the network: 21 November 1948

Chiswick Park (known as Acton Green from 1879–87 and Chiswick Park & Acton Green from 1887–1910)
Line(s) served: District
Opened: 1 July 1879

Chorleywood (known as Chorley Wood & Chenies from 1915–34)
Line(s) served: Metropolitan
Opened: 8 July 1889

Clapham Common
Line(s) served: Northern
Opened: 3 June 1900

Clapham North (known as Clapham Road from 1900–26)
Line(s) served: Northern
Opened: 3 June 1900

Clapham South
Line(s) served: Northern
Opened: 13 September 1926

Cockfosters
Line(s) served: Piccadilly
Opened: 31 July 1933

Colindale
Line(s) served: Northern
Opened: 18 August 1924

Colliers Wood
Line(s) served: Northern
Opened: 13 September 1926

Covent Garden
Line(s) served: Piccadilly
Opened: 11 April 1907

Crossharbour & London Arena (known as Crossharbour from 1987–1994)
Line(s) served: DLR
Opened: 31 August 1987

Croxley (known as Croxley Green from 1925–49)
Line(s) served: Metropolitan
Opened: 2 November 1925

Custom House
Line(s) served: DLR
First connected to the network: 28 March 1994

Cutty Sark
Line(s) served: DLR
Opened: 20 November 1999

Cyprus
Line(s) served: DLR
Opened: 28 March 1994

Dagenham East (known as Dagenham from 1888–1949)
Line(s) served: District
First connected to the network: 2 June 1902

Dagenham Heathway (known as Heathway from 1932–1949)
Line(s) served: District
Opened: 12 September 1932

Debden
Line(s) served: Central
First connected to the network: 25 September 1949

Deptford Bridge
Line(s) served: DLR
Opened: 20 November 1999

Devons Road
Line(s) served: DLR
Opened: 31 August 1987

Dollis Hill
Line(s) served: Jubilee
Opened: 1 October 1909

Ealing Broadway
Line(s) served: Central, District
First connected to the network: 1 July 1879

Ealing Common (known as Ealing Common & West Acton from 1886–1910)
Line(s) served: District, Piccadilly
Opened: 1 July 1879

Earl's Court
Line(s) served: District, Piccadilly
Opened: 30 October 1871 (relocated on 1 February 1878)

East Acton
Line(s) served: Central
Opened: 3 August 1920

East Finchley
Line(s) served: Northern
First connected to the network: 3 July 1939

East Ham
Line(s) served: District, Hammersmith & City
First connected to the network: 2 June 1902

East India
Line(s) served: DLR
Opened: 28 March 1994

East Putney
Line(s) served: District
Opened: 3 June 1889

Eastcote
Line(s) served: Metropolitan, Piccadilly
Opened: 26 May 1906

Edgware
Line(s) served: Northern
Opened: 18 August 1924

Edgware Road (Circle, District, Hammersmith & City)
Line(s) served: Circle, District, Hammersmith & City
Opened: 1 October 1863

Edgware Road (Bakerloo)
Line(s) served: Bakerloo
Opened: 15 June 1907

Elephant & Castle
Line(s) served: Bakerloo, Northern
Opened: 18 December 1890

Elm Park
Line(s) served: District
Opened: 13 May 1935

Elverson Road
Line(s) served: DLR
Opened: 20 November 1999

Embankment (known as Charing Cross on the District line from 1870–1915, Charing Cross (Embankment) on the Bakerloo and Northern lines from 1914–15 and Charing Cross Embankment from 1974–6)
Line(s) served: Bakerloo, Circle, District, Northern
Opened: 30 May 1870

Epping
Line(s) served: Central
First connected to the network: 25 September 1949

Euston
Line(s) served: Northern, Victoria
Opened: 22 June 1907

Euston Square (known as Gower Street from 1863–1909)
Line(s) served: Circle, Hammersmith & City, Metropolitan
Opened: 10 January 1863

Fairlop
Line(s) served: Central
First connected to the network: 31 May 1948

Farringdon (known as Farringdon Street from 1863–1922 and Farringdon & High Holborn from 1922–36)
Line(s) served: Circle, Hammersmith & City, Metropolitan
Opened: 10 January 1863 (relocated 23 December 1865)

Finchley Central
Line(s) served: Northern
First connected to the network: 14 April 1940

Finchley Road
Line(s) served: Jubilee, Metropolitan
Opened: 30 June 1879

Finsbury Park
Line(s) served: Piccadilly, Victoria
First connected to the network: 14 February 1904

Fulham Broadway (known as Walham Green from 1880–1952)
Line(s) served: District
Opened: 1 March 1880

Gallions Reach
Line(s) served: DLR
Opened: 28 March 1994

Gants Hill
Line(s) served: Central
Opened: 14 December 1947

Gloucester Road (known as Brompton (Gloucester Road) from 1868–1907)
Line(s) served: Circle, District, Piccadilly
Opened: 1 October 1868

Golders Green
Line(s) served: Northern
Opened: 22 June 1907

Goldhawk Road
Line(s) served: Circle, Hammersmith & City
Opened: 1 April 1914

Goodge Street (known as Tottenham Court Road from 1907–08)
Line(s) served: Northern
Opened: 22 June 1907

Grange Hill
Line(s) served: Central
First connected to the network: 21 November 1948

Great Portland Street (known as Portland Road from 1863–1917 and Great Portland Street & Regent's Park from 1923–33)
Line(s) served: Circle, Hammersmith & City, Metropolitan
Opened: 10 January 1863

Greenford
Line(s) served: Central
First connected to the network: 30 June 1947

Green Park (known as Dover Street from 1906–33)
Line(s) served: Jubilee, Piccadilly, Victoria
Opened: 15 December 1906

Greenwich
Line(s) served: DLR
First connected to the network: 20 November 1999

Gunnersbury
Line(s) served: District
First connected to the network: 1 June 1877

Hainault
Line(s) served: Central
First connected to the network: 31 May 1948

Hammersmith (Circle, Hammersmith & City)
Line(s) served: Circle, Hammersmith & City
Opened: 13 June 1864 (relocated) 1 December 1868

Hammersmith (District, Piccadilly)
Line(s) served: District, Piccadilly
Opened: 9 September 1874

Hampstead
Line(s) served: Northern
Opened: 22 June 1907

Hanger Lane
Line(s) served: Central
Opened: 30 June 1947

Harlesden
Line(s) served: Bakerloo
First connected to the network: 16 April 1917

Harrow & Wealdstone
Line(s) served: Bakerloo
First connected to the network: 16 April 1917

Harrow-on-the-Hill (known as Harrow from 1880–94)
Line(s) served: Metropolitan
Opened: 2 August 1880

Hatton Cross
Line(s) served: Piccadilly
Opened: 19 July 1975

Heathrow Terminals 1, 2, 3 (known as Heathrow Central from 1977–83 and Heathrow Central Terminals 1, 2, 3 from 1983–86)
Line(s) served: Piccadilly
Opened: 16 December 1977

Heathrow Terminal 4
Line(s) served: Piccadilly
Opened: 12 April 1986

Heathrow Terminal 5
Line(s) served: Piccadilly
Opened: 27 March 2008

Hendon Central
Line(s) served: Northern
Opened: 19 November 1923

Heron Quays
Line(s) served: DLR
Opened: 31 August 1987

High Barnet
Line(s) served: Northern
First connected to the network: 14 April 1940

Highbury & Islington
Line(s) served: Victoria
First connected to the network: 1 September 1968

Highgate
Line(s) served: Northern
First connected to the network: 19 January 1941

High Street Kensington
Line(s) served: Circle, District
Opened: 1 October 1868

Hillingdon (known as Hillingdon (Swakeleys) from 1934–50s)
Line(s) served: Metropolitan, Piccadilly
Opened: 10 December 1923 (relocated 6 December 1992)

Holborn (known as Holborn (Kingsway) from 1906–60s)
Line(s) served: Central, Piccadilly
Opened: 15 December 1906

Holland Park
Line(s) served: Central
Opened: 30 July 1900

Holloway Road
Line(s) served: Piccadilly
Opened: 15 December 1906

Hornchurch
Line(s) served: District
First connected to the network: 2 June 1902

Hounslow Central (known as Heston Hounslow from 1886–1925)
Line(s) served: Piccadilly
Opened: 1 April 1886

Hounslow East (known as Hounslow Town from 1909–25)
Line(s) served: Piccadilly
Opened: 2 May 1909

Hounslow West (known as Hounslow Barracks from 1884–1925)
Line(s) served: Piccadilly
Opened: 21 July 1884

Hyde Park Corner
Line(s) served: Piccadilly
Opened: 15 December 1906

Ickenham
Line(s) served: Metropolitan, Piccadilly
Opened: 25 September 1905

Island Gardens
Line(s) served: DLR
Opened: 31 August 1987 (relocated 20 November 1999)

Kennington
Line(s) served: Northern
Opened: 18 December 1890

Kensal Green
Line(s) served: Bakerloo
Opened: 1 October 1916

Kensington (Olympia) (known as Kensington (Addison Road) from 1868–1946)
Line(s) served: District
First connected to the network: 1 July 1864

Kentish Town
Line(s) served: Northern
First connected to the network: 22 June 1907

Kenton
Line(s) served: Bakerloo
First connected to the network: 16 April 1917

Kew Gardens
Line(s) served: District
First connected to the network: 1 June 1877

Kilburn (known as Kilburn & Brondesbury from 1879–1950)
Line(s) served: Jubilee
Opened: 24 November 1879

Kilburn Park
Line(s) served: Bakerloo
Opened: 31 January 1915

Kingsbury
Line(s) served: Jubilee
Opened: 10 December 1932

King George V
Line(s) served: DLR
Opened: 22 December 2005

King's Cross St Pancras
Line(s) served: Circle, Hammersmith & City, Metropolitan, Northern, Piccadilly, Victoria
First connected to the network: 10 January 1863 (Metropolitan line relocated 9 March 1941)

Knightsbridge
Line(s) served: Piccadilly
Opened: 15 December 1906

Ladbroke Grove (known as Notting Hill from 1864–80, Notting Hill & Ladbroke Grove from 1880–1919 and Ladbroke Grove (North Kensington) from 1919–38)
Line(s) served: Circle, Hammersmith & City
Opened: 13 June 1864

Lambeth North (known as Kennington Road in 1906 and Westminster Bridge Road from 1906–17)
Line(s) served: Bakerloo
Opened: 10 March 1906

Lancaster Gate
Line(s) served: Central
Opened: 30 July 1900

Langdon Park
Line(s) served: DLR
Opened: 9 December 2007

Latimer Road
Line(s) served: Circle, Hammersmith & City
Opened: 16 December 1868

Leicester Square
Line(s) served: Northern, Piccadilly
Opened: 15 December 1906

Lewisham
Line(s) served: DLR
First connected to the network: 20 November 1999

Leyton
Line(s) served: Central
First connected to the network: 5 May 1947

Leytonstone
Line(s) served: Central
First connected to the network: 5 May 1947

Limehouse
Line(s) served: DLR
First connected to the network: 31 August 1987

Liverpool Street (known as Bishopsgate from 1875–1909)
Line(s) served: Central, Circle, Hammersmith & City, Metropolitan
First connected to the network: 1 February 1875 (relocated 12 July 1875)

London Bridge
Line(s) served: Jubilee, Northern
First connected to the network: 25 February 1900

London City Airport
Line(s) served: DLR
Opened: 22 December 2005

Loughton
Line(s) served: Central
First connected to the network: 21 November 1948

Maida Vale
Line(s) served: Bakerloo
Opened: 6 June 1915

Manor House
Line(s) served: Piccadilly
Opened: 19 September 1932

Mansion House
Line(s) served: Circle, District
Opened: 3 July 1871

Marble Arch
Line(s) served: Central
Opened: 30 July 1900

Marylebone (known as Great Central from 1907–17)
Line(s) served: Bakerloo
First connected to the network: 27 March 1907

Mile End
Line(s) served: Central, District, Hammersmith & City
Opened: 2 June 1902

Mill Hill East
Line(s) served: Northern
First connected to the network: 18 May 1941

Monument (known as East Cheap in 1884)
Line(s) served: Circle, District
Opened: 6 October 1884

Moorgate (known as Moorgate Street on the Metropolitan line from 1865–1924)
Line(s) served: Circle, Hammersmith & City, Metropolitan, Northern
Opened: 23 December 1865

Moor Park (known as Sandy Lodge from 1910–23 and Moor Park & Sandy Lodge from 1923–50)
Line(s) served: Metropolitan
Opened: 9 May 1910

Morden
Line(s) served: Northern
Opened: 13 September 1926

Mornington Crescent
Line(s) served: Northern
Opened: 22 June 1907

Mudchute
Line(s) served: DLR
First connected to the network: 31 August 1987 (relocated 20 November 1999)

Neasden (known as Kingsbury & Neasden from 1880–1910 and Neasden & Kingsbury from 1910–32)
Line(s) served: Jubilee
Opened: 2 August 1880

Newbury Park
Line(s) served: Central
First connected to the network: 14 December 1947

North Acton
Line(s) served: Central
First connected to the network: 5 November 1923

North Ealing
Line(s) served: Piccadilly
Opened: 23 June 1903

North Greenwich
Line(s) served: Jubilee
Opened: 14 May 1999

North Harrow
Line(s) served: Metropolitan
Opened: 22 March 1915

North Wembley
Line(s) served: Bakerloo
First connected to the network: 16 April 1917

Northfields (known as Northfield Halt from 1908–11 and Northfields & Little Ealing from 1911–32)
Line(s) served: Piccadilly
Opened: 16 April 1908 (relocated 19 May 1932)

Northolt
Line(s) served: Central
First connected to the network: 21 November 1948

Northwick Park (known as Northwick Park & Kenton from 1923–33)
Line(s) served: Metropolitan
Opened: 28 June 1923

Northwood
Line(s) served: Metropolitan
Opened: 1 September 1887

Northwood Hills
Line(s) served: Metropolitan
Opened: 13 November 1933

Notting Hill Gate
Line(s) served: Central, Circle, District
Opened: 1 October 1868

Oakwood (known as Enfield West from 1933–34 and Enfield West (Oakwood) from 1934–46)
Line(s) served: Piccadilly
Opened: 13 March 1933

Old Street
Line(s) served: Northern
Opened: 17 November 1901

Osterley (known as Osterley & Spring Grove from 1883–1934)
Line(s) served: Piccadilly
Opened: 1 May 1883 (relocated 25 March 1934)

Oval (known as The Oval from 1890–94)
Line(s) served: Northern
Opened: 18 December 1890

Oxford Circus
Line(s) served: Bakerloo, Central, Victoria
Opened: 30 July 1900

Paddington (known as Paddington (Bishop's Road) on the Hammersmith & City line from 1863–1933 and Paddington (Praed Street) on the Circle line from 1868–1948)
Line(s) served: Bakerloo, Circle, District, Hammersmith & City
First connected to the network: 10 January 1863

Park Royal (known as Park Royal & Twyford Abbey from 1903–31 and Park Royal (Hanger Hill) from 1936–47)
Line(s) served: Piccadilly
Opened: 23 June 1903 (relocated 6 July 1931)

Parsons Green
Line(s) served: District
Opened: 1 March 1880

Perivale
Line(s) served: Central
First connected to the network: 30 June 1947

Piccadilly Circus
Line(s) served: Bakerloo, Piccadilly
Opened: 10 March 1906

Pimlico
Line(s) served: Victoria
Opened: 14 September 1972

Pinner
Line(s) served: Metropolitan
Opened: 25 May 1885

Plaistow
Line(s) served: District, Hammersmith & City
First connected to the network: 2 June 1902

Pontoon Dock
Line(s) served: DLR
Opened: 22 December 2005

Poplar
Line(s) served: DLR
Opened: 31 August 1987

Preston Road
Line(s) served: Metropolitan
Opened: 21 May 1908 (relocated 3 January 1932)

Prince Regent
Line(s) served: DLR
Opened: 28 March 1994

Pudding Mill Lane
Line(s) served: DLR
Opened: 1 February 1996

Putney Bridge (known as Putney Bridge & Fulham from 1880–1902
and Putney Bridge & Hurlingham from 1902–32)
Line(s) served: District
Opened: 1 March 1880

Queen's Park
Line(s) served: Bakerloo
First connected to the network: 11 February 1915

Queensbury
Line(s) served: Jubilee
Opened: 16 December 1934

Queensway (known as Queen's Road from 1900–46)
Line(s) served: Central
Opened: 30 July 1900

Ravenscourt Park (known as Shaftesbury Road from 1877–88)
Line(s) served: District
First connected to the network: 1 June 1877

Rayners Lane
Line(s) served: Metropolitan, Piccadilly
Opened: 26 May 1906

Redbridge
Line(s) served: Central
Opened: 14 December 1947

Regent's Park
Line(s) served: Bakerloo
Opened: 10 March 1906

Richmond
Line(s) served: District
First connected to the network: 1 June 1877

Rickmansworth
Line(s) served: Metropolitan
Opened: 1 September 1887

Roding Valley
Line(s) served: Central
First connected to the network: 21 November 1948

Royal Albert
Line(s) served: DLR
Opened: 28 March 1994

Royal Oak
Line(s) served: Circle, Hammersmith & City
First connected to the network: 30 October 1871

Royal Victoria
Line(s) served: DLR
Opened: 28 March 1994

Ruislip
Line(s) served: Metropolitan, Piccadilly
Opened: 4 July 1904

Ruislip Gardens
Line(s) served: Central
First connected to the network: 29 November 1948

Ruislip Manor
Line(s) served: Metropolitan, Piccadilly
Opened: 5 August 1912

Russell Square
Line(s) served: Piccadilly
Opened: 15 December 1906

St James's Park
Line(s) served: Circle, District
Opened: 24 December 1868

St John's Wood
Line(s) served: Jubilee
Opened: 20 November 1939

St Paul's (known as Post Office from 1900–37)
Line(s) served: Central
Opened: 30 July 1900

Seven Sisters
Line(s) served: Victoria
First connected to the network: 1 September 1968

Shadwell
Line(s) served: DLR, East London
Opened: 31 August 1876

Shepherd's Bush
Line(s) served: Central
Opened: 30 July 1900

Shepherd's Bush Market (known as Shepherd's Bush from 1864–2008)
Line(s) served: Circle, Hammersmith & City
Opened: 13 June 1864 (relocated 1 April 1914)

Sloane Square
Line(s) served: Circle, District
Opened: 24 December 1868

Snaresbrook
Line(s) served: Central
First connected to the network: 14 December 1947

South Ealing
Line(s) served: Piccadilly
Opened: 1 May 1883

South Harrow
Line(s) served: Piccadilly
Opened: 28 June 1903 (relocated 5 July 1935)

South Kensington
Line(s) served: Circle, District, Piccadilly
Opened: 24 December 1868

South Kenton
Line(s) served: Bakerloo
Opened: 3 July 1933

South Quay
Line(s) served: DLR
Opened: 31 August 1987 (relocated 26 October 2009)

South Ruislip
Line(s) served: Central
First connected to the network: 23 November 1948

South Wimbledon (known as South Wimbledon (Merton) from 1928–phased out)
Line(s) served: Northern
Opened: 13 September 1926

South Woodford (known as South Woodford (George Lane) from 1947–50)
Line(s) served: Central
First connected to the network: 14 December 1947

Southfields
Line(s) served: District
Opened: 3 June 1889

Southgate
Line(s) served: Piccadilly
Opened: 13 March 1933

Southwark
Line(s) served: Jubilee
Opened: 24 September 1999

Stamford Brook
Line(s) served: District
First connected to the network: 1 February 1912

Stanmore
Line(s) served: Jubilee
Opened: 10 December 1932

Star Lane
Line(s) served: DLR
Opened: 31 August 2011

Stepney Green
Line(s) served: District, Hammersmith & City
Opened: 23 June 1902

Stockwell
Line(s) served: Northern, Victoria
Opened: 18 December 1890

Stonebridge Park
Line(s) served: Bakerloo
First connected to the network: 16 April 1917

Stratford
Line(s) served: Central, DLR, Jubilee
First connected to the network: 4 December 1946

Stratford High Street
Line(s) served: DLR
First connected to the network: 31 August 2011

Stratford International
Line(s) served: DLR
Opened: 31 August 2011

Sudbury Hill
Line(s) served: Piccadilly
Opened: 28 June 1903

Sudbury Town
Line(s) served: Piccadilly
Opened: 28 June 1903

Swiss Cottage
Line(s) served: Jubilee
Opened: 20 November 1939

Temple
Line(s) served: Circle, District
Opened: 30 May 1870

Theydon Bois
Line(s) served: Central
First connected to the network: 25 September 1949

Tooting Bec (known as Trinity Road (Tooting Bec) from 1926–50)
Line(s) served: Northern
Opened: 13 September 1926

Tooting Broadway
Line(s) served: Northern
Opened: 13 September 1926

Tottenham Court Road (known as Oxford Street on the Northern line from 1907–08)
Line(s) served: Central, Northern
Opened: 30 July 1900

Tottenham Hale
Line(s) served: Victoria
First connected to the network: 1 September 1968

Totteridge & Whetstone
Line(s) served: Northern
First connected to the network: 14 April 1940

Tower Gateway
Line(s) served: DLR
Opened: 31 August 1987

Tower Hill (known as Tower of London from 1882–84 and Mark Lane from 1884–1946)
Line(s) served: Circle, District
Opened: 25 September 1882 (relocated in 12 October 1884 and 5 February 1967)

Tufnell Park
Line(s) served: Northern
Opened: 22 June 1907

Turnham Green
Line(s) served: District, Piccadilly
First connected to the network: 1 June 1877

Turnpike Lane
Line(s) served: Piccadilly
Opened: 19 September 1932

Upminster
Line(s) served: District
First connected to the network: 2 June 1902

Upminster Bridge
Line(s) served: District
First connected to the network: 2 June 1902

Upney
Line(s) served: District
Opened: 12 September 1932

Upton Park
Line(s) served: District, Hammersmith & City
First connected to the network: 2 June 1902

Uxbridge
Line(s) served: Metropolitan, Piccadilly
Opened: 4 July 1904 (relocated 4 December 1938)

Vauxhall
Line(s) served: Victoria
First connected to the network: 23 July 1971

Victoria
Line(s) served: Circle, District, Victoria
First connected to the network: 24 December 1868

Walthamstow Central
Line(s) served: Victoria
First connected to the network: 1 September 1968

Wanstead
Line(s) served: Central
Opened: 14 December 1947

Warren Street (known as Euston Road from 1907–08)
Line(s) served: Northern, Victoria
Opened: 22 June 1907

Warwick Avenue
Line(s) served: Bakerloo
Opened: 31 January 1915

Waterloo
Line(s) served: Bakerloo, Jubilee, Northern, Waterloo & City
First connected to the network: 10 March 1906

Watford
Line(s) served: Metropolitan
Opened: 2 November 1925

Wembley Central (known as Wembley for Sudbury from 1917–48)
Line(s) served: Bakerloo
First connected to the network: 16 April 1917

Wembley Park
Line(s) served: Jubilee, Metropolitan
Opened: 12 May 1894

West Acton
Line(s) served: Central
Opened: 5 November 1923

West Brompton
Line(s) served: District
First connected to the network: 12 April 1869

West Finchley
Line(s) served: Northern
First connected to the network: 14 April 1940

West Ham (known as West Ham (Manor Road) from 1924–69)
Line(s) served: District, DLR, Hammersmith & City, Jubilee
First connected to the network: 2 June 1902

West Hampstead
Line(s) served: Jubilee
Opened: 30 June 1879

West Harrow
Line(s) served: Metropolitan
Opened: 17 November 1913

West India Quay
Line(s) served: DLR
Opened: 31 August 1987

West Kensington (known as North End (Fulham) from 1874–77)
Line(s) served: District
Opened: 9 September 1874

West Ruislip
Line(s) served: Central
First connected to the network: 21 November 1948

West Silvertown
Line(s) served: DLR
Opened: 22 December 2005

Westbourne Park
Line(s) served: Circle, Hammersmith & City
Opened: 1 February 1866 (relocated 1 November 1871)

Westferry
Line(s) served: DLR
Opened: 31 August 1987

Westminster (known as Westminster Bridge from 1868–1907)
Line(s) served: Circle, District, Jubilee
Opened: 24 December 1868

White City
Line(s) served: Central
Opened: 23 November 1947

Whitechapel (known as Whitechapel (Mile End) from 1884–1901)
Line(s) served: District, East London, Hammersmith & City
Opened: 1 October 1876

Willesden Green
Line(s) served: Jubilee
Opened: 24 November 1879

Willesden Junction
Line(s) served: Bakerloo
First connected to the network: 10 May 1915

Wimbledon
Line(s) served: District
First connected to the network: 3 June 1889

Wimbledon Park
Line(s) served: District
Opened: 3 June 1889

Wood Green
Line(s) served: Piccadilly
Opened: 19 September 1932

Wood Lane
Line(s) served: Circle, Hammersmith and City
Opened: 12 October 2008

Woodford
Line(s) served: Central
First connected to the network: 14 December 1947

Woodside Park
Line(s) served: Northern
First connected to the network: 12 April 1940

Woolwich Arsenal
Line(s) served: DLR
First connected to the network: 10 January 2009

APPENDIX 2: LONDON UNDERGROUND STATIONS NO LONGER ON THE NETWORK

Alphabetical list, including dates of beginning and ceasing service, and lines served.

Aldwych (known as Strand from 1907–15)
Line(s) served: Piccadilly
Opened: 30 November 1907
What happened? Station closed on 30 September 1994

Aylesbury
Line(s) served: Metropolitan
First connected to the network: 1892
What happened? London Underground services ceased on 10 September 1961

Blake Hall
Line(s) served: Central
Opened: 24 April 1865
What happened? Station closed on 2 November 1981

Brill
Line(s) served: Metropolitan
First connected to the network: 1 July 1891
What happened? Station closed on 30 November 1935

British Museum
Line(s) served: Central
Opened: 30 July 1900
What happened? Station closed on 24 September 1933

Brompton Road
Line(s) served: Piccadilly
Opened: 15 December 1906
What happened? Station closed on 29 July 1934

Bushey
Line(s) served: Bakerloo
First connected to the network: 16 April 1917
What happened? London Underground services ceased on 24 September 1982

Carpenders Park
Line(s) served: Bakerloo
Opened: 16 April 1917
What happened? London Underground services ceased on 24 September 1982

Castle Hill (Ealing Dean)
Line(s) served: District
First connected to the network: 1 March 1883
What happened? London Underground services ceased on 30 September 1885

City Road
Line(s) served: Northern
Opened: 17 November 1901
What happened? Station closed on 8 August 1922

Down Street
Line(s) served: Piccadilly
Opened: 15 March 1907
What happened? Station closed on 21 May 1932

Drayton Park
Line(s) served: Northern
First connected to the network: 1913
What happened? London Underground services ceased on 4 October 1975

Essex Road
Line(s) served: Northern
First connected to the network: 1933
What happened? London Underground services ceased on 3 October 1975

Granborough Road
Line(s) served: Metropolitan
First connected to the network: 1868
What happened? London Underground services ceased on 4 July 1936

Great Missenden
Line(s) served: Metropolitan
Opened: 1 September 1892
What happened? London Underground services ceased on 10 September 1961

Grove Road (Hammersmith)
Line(s) served: Metropolitan
Opened: 1 January 1869
What happened? London Underground services ceased on 31 December 1906

Hanwell
Line(s) served: District
First connected to the network: 1 March 1883
What happened? London Underground services ceased on 30 September 1885

Hatch End (known as Pinner & Hatch End from 1917–1920 and Hatch End (for Pinner) from 1920–1956)
Line(s) served: Bakerloo
First connected to the network: 16 April 1917
What happened? London Underground services ceased on 24 September 1982

Hayes
Line(s) served: District
First connected to the network: 1 March 1883
What happened? London Underground services ceased on 30 September 1885

Headstone Lane
Line(s) served: Bakerloo
Opened: 16 April 1917
What happened? London Underground services ceased on 24 September 1982

King William Street
Line(s) served: Northern
Opened: 18 December 1890
What happened? Station closed on 24 February 1900 and replaced by Bank

Langley
Line(s) served: District
First connected to the network: 1 March 1883
What happened? London Underground services ceased on 30 September 1885

Leigh-on-Sea
Line(s) served: District
First connected to the network: 1911
What happened? London Underground services ceased on 30 September 1939

Lord's (known as St John's Wood Road from 1868–1925 and St John's Wood from 1925–1939)
Line(s) served: Metropolitan
Opened: 1868
What happened? Station closed on 19 November 1939

Marlborough Road
Line(s) served: Metropolitan
Opened: 1868
What happened? Station closed on 19 November 1939

New Cross
Line(s) served: East London
First connected to the network: 1 October 1884
What happened? London Underground services ceased on 22 December 2007; service now operated by London Overground

New Cross Gate
Line(s) served: East London
First connected to the network: 1 October 1884
What happened? London Underground services ceased on 22 December 2007; service now operated by London Overground

North Weald
Line(s) served: Central
First connected to the network: 25 September 1949
What happened? Station closed on 30 September 1994 (now part of the Epping Ongar Railway attraction)

Ongar
Line(s) served: Central
First connected to the network: 25 September 1949
What happened? Station closed on 30 September 1994 (now part of the Epping Ongar Railway attraction)

Quainton Road
Line(s) served: Metropolitan
First connected to the network: 1891
What happened? London Underground services ceased on 5 July 1936

Rotherhithe
Line(s) served: East London
First connected to the network: 1 October 1884
What happened? London Underground services ceased on 22 December 2007; service now operated by London Overground

St Mary's (Whitechapel Road)
Line(s) served: District
Opened: 3 March 1884
What happened? Station closed on 30 April 1938

Shoeburyness
Line(s) served: District
First connected to the network: 1911
What happened? London Underground services ceased on 30 September 1939

Shoreditch High Street (known as Shoreditch from 1869-2006)
Line(s) served: East London
First connected to the network: 31 March 1913
Closed: 9 June 2006 (replaced by Shoreditch High Street on the London Overground)

Slough
Line(s) served: District
First connected to the network: 1 March 1883
What happened? London Underground services ceased on 30 September 1885

South Acton
Line(s) served: District
First connected to the network: 13 June 1905
What happened? London Underground services ceased on 28 February 1959

Southend Central
Line(s) served: District
First connected to the network: 1 June 1910
What happened? London Underground services ceased on 30 September 1939

Southall
Line(s) served: District
First connected to the network: 1 March 1883
What happened? London Underground services ceased on 30 September 1885

South Kentish Town
Line(s) served: Northern
Opened: 22 June 1907
What happened? Station closed on 5 June 1924

Stoke Mandeville
Line(s) served: Metropolitan
Opened: 1 September 1892
What happened? London Underground services ceased on 10 September 1961

Surrey Quays (known as Deptford Road from 1869–1911 and Surrey Docks from 1911–1989)
Line(s) served: East London
First connected to the network: 1 October 1884
What happened? London Underground services ceased on 22 December 2007; service now operated by London Overground

Uxbridge Road
Line(s) served: Metropolitan
Opened: 1 November 1869
What happened? Station closed on 21 October 1940

Verney Junction
Line(s) served: Metropolitan
First connected to the network: 1 July 1891
What happened? London Underground services ceased on 6 July 1936

Waddesdon (known as Waddesdon Manor from 1897–1922)
Line(s) served: Metropolitan
Opened: 1 January 1897
What happened? Station closed on 5 July 1936

Waddesdon Road (known as Waddesdon from 1899–1922)
Line(s) served: Metropolitan
First connected to the network: 1 December 1899
What happened? Station closed: 30 November 1935

Wapping (known as Wapping & Shadwell from 1869–1876)
Line(s) served: East London
First connected to the network: 1 October 1884
What happened? London Underground services ceased on 22 December 2007; service now operated by London Overground

Watford High Street
Line(s) served: Bakerloo
First connected to the network: 1917
Closed: 24 September 1982

Watford Junction
Line(s) served: Bakerloo
What happened? London Underground services ceased on 24 September 1982

Wendover
Line(s) served: Metropolitan
Opened: 1 September 1892
What happened? London Underground services ceased on 10 September 1961

Westcott
Line(s) served: Metropolitan
First connected to the network: 1899
What happened? Station closed on 30 November 1935

West Drayton
Line(s) served: District
First connected to the network: 1 March 1883
What happened? London Underground services ceased on 30 September 1885

Windsor
Line(s) served: District
First connected to the network: 1 March 1883
What happened? London Underground services ceased on 30 September 1885

Winslow Road
Line(s) served: Metropolitan
First connected to the network: 1 July 1891
What happened? London Underground services ceased on 4 July 1936

Wood Lane
Line(s) served: Central
Opened: 1908
What happened? Station closed in 1947

Wood Siding
Line(s) served: Metropolitan
First connected to the network: 1899
What happened? Station closed on 30 November 1935

Wotton
Line(s) served: Metropolitan
First connected to the network: 1899
What happened? Station closed on 30 November 1935

York Road
Line(s) served: Piccadilly
Opened: 15 December 1906
What happened? Station closed on 17 September 1932

APPENDIX 3: LONDON UNDERGROUND RAILWAY COMPANIES

Baker Street & Waterloo Railway
Formed: 1893
What happened? After struggling financially, in 1902 the BS&WR became a subsidiary of the Underground Electric Railways Company of London (UERL).

Brompton & Piccadilly Circus Railway
Formed: 1896
What happened? Due to financial constraints, in 1902 the B&PCR merged with the Great Northern & Strand Railway to become the Great Northern, Piccadilly & Brompton Railway and became a subsidiary of the UERL.

Central London Railway
Formed: 1889
What happened? Secured funding six years after it was established and was taken over by the UERL in 1913.

Charing Cross, Euston & Hampstead Railway
Formed: 1891
What happened? Became a subsidiary of the UERL in 1900 after construction was delayed due to lack of funding. Merged with the City & South London Railway in the 1920s to form the Northern line.

City & South London Railway
Formed: 1883
What happened? Became a subsidiary of UERL in 1913 and was merged with the Charing Cross, Euston & Hampstead Railway in the 1920s to form the Northern line.

East London Railway
Formed: 1865
What happened? Became part of the London Passenger Transport Board (often just referred to as London Transport) in 1933, along with the other railway companies under the UERL.

Edgware, Highgate & London Railway
Formed: 1862
What happened? Taken under the control of the Great Northern Railway in 1867. GNR came under ownership of the London & North Eastern Railway in 1923.

Great Northern & City Railway
Formed: 1898
What happened? Merged with the Brompton & Piccadilly Circus Railway in 1902 to form the Great Northern, Piccadilly & Brompton Railway and became a subsidiary of the UERL.

Hammersmith & City Railway
Formed: 1864
What happened? Hammersmith & City services originally operated on the Metropolitan Railway lines and the line was only shown separately on Tube maps from 1988. The company came under the ownership of the LPTB in 1934.

Metropolitan & Great Central Joint Railway
Formed: 1906
What happened? Joint venture from the Metropolitan Railway and the Great Central Railway; took over the Metropolitan routes to the north and west of South Harrow Junction. In 1923 the GCR came under the ownership of London & North Eastern Railway (although the M&GCJR retained its title) and, in 1933, the Metropolitan was taken under the LPTB umbrella.

Metropolitan & St John's Wood Railway
Formed: 1868
What happened? This was an extension of the Metropolitan Railway, heading north-west to the suburbs; it was absorbed by the Metropolitan Railway in 1882.

Metropolitan Inner Circle Completion Railway Company
Formed: 1874
What happened? Company formed by city financiers frustrated with the lack of progress on the Inner Circle line. Oversaw works until completion and then disbanded.

Metropolitan Railway
Formed: 1863
What happened? Became part of the London Passenger Transport Board in 1933, along with the railway companies under the UERL banner, and the city's bus and tram operators.

Metropolitan District Railway
Formed: 1864
What happened? Along with the UERL and the Metropolitan Railway, in 1933 the MDR became part of the London Passenger Transport Board.

Waterloo & City Railway
Formed: 1898
What happened? Originally operated by the London & South Western Railway; absorbed by the Southern Railway in 1923; came under ownership of British Rail under nationalisation of 1948; only transferred to the London Underground network in 1994.

Whitechapel & Bow Railway
Formed: 1902
What happened? Joint venture from the Metropolitan District Railway and the London, Tilbury & Southend Railway; came under the ownership of the London, Midland & Scottish Railway in 1923; passed on to London Transport under nationalisation in 1948.

RESOURCES

BOOKS

Non-fiction

Brandon, David and Brooke, Alan, *Haunted London Underground* (The History Press, 2009).
You'll never walk the platforms of certain stations quite so nonchalantly again; a comprehensive guide to the mystery and supposed hauntings surrounding many a London Underground station.

Chernaik, Judith (Ed.), *Poems on the Underground: A New Edition* (Particular Books, 2012).
A new edition of the Poems on the Underground series, released to celebrate the 150th anniversary of the Tube.

Dobbin, Claire, *London Underground Maps* (Lund Humphries, 2012).
A collection of maps dating back to 1900, showing the evolution of the Tube and its diagrammatic map design.

Glover, John, *London's Underground* (Ian Allan Publishing, 2010). Regularly published for more than 50 years, this offers a comprehensive guide to the history of the Underground and is routinely updated to take in changes to the system.

Halliday, Stephen, *Underground to Everywhere: London's Underground Railway in the Life of the Capital* (The History Press, 2004).
A humorous insight into the history of the London Underground and the characters that brought it into being.

Martin, Andrew, *Underground, Overground: A Passenger's History of the Tube* (Profile Books, 2012).
Incredibly insightful read from the point of view of a seasoned passenger and railway-themed crime novelist.

Mason, Mark, *Walk the Lines: The London Underground, Overground* (Random House, 2011).
Mason rediscovers London by walking the routes of the Tube lines overground – incredibly informative and entertaining.

Pedroche, Ben, *Do Not Alight Here: Walking London's Lost Underground & Railway Stations* (Capital Transport Publishing, 2011).
A wealth of information about London's abandoned, forgotten and never-opened stations, along with walking routes to see what remains of them.

Revill, David, *London By Tube: A History of Underground Station Names* (Fast Fish Publications, 2011).
Ever wondered why the station/area was called Blackfriars? Seven Sisters? Brent Cross? Well wonder no more…

Ross, Christopher, *Tunnel Visions: Journeys of an Underground Philosopher* (Fourth Estate, 2002).
A glimpse into the life of a London Underground station assistant, as a philosopher dons a hi-vis vest and takes up employment on a bustling Victoria line platform for a year.

Smith, Stephen, *Underground London: Beneath the City Streets* (Abacus, 2005).
Embark on a journey through subterranean London, through tunnels and sewers, crypts and passages, there's plenty to be learnt here.

Wolmar, Christian, *The Subterranean Railway: How the London Underground Was Built and How it Changed the City Forever* (Atlantic Books, 2012, 2nd ed.).
Updated version of this popular book – an in-depth insight into the history of the Tube and how it helped build the city around it.

Fiction

Gaiman, Neil, *Neverwhere* (Headline Review, 2005).
Spawned from the TV series of the same name, the book takes us deeper into the dark, dank tunnels and the alternate worlds both above and below London.

Lowe, Keith, *Tunnel Vision* (Arrow Books, 2001).
The story of a soon-to-be-groom who attempts to visit every station on the Underground the day before his wedding.

Macken, John, *Breaking Point* (Corgi, 2009).
Sci-fi crime thriller where we find a homicidal maniac is loose on the London Underground.

Oliver, Jonathan (Ed.), *The End of the Line* (Solaris, 2010).
A creepy collection of contemporary short horror stories, all set below ground – on the London Underground and subterranean railway networks beneath other cities around the world.

Simmons, John; Taylor, Neil; Rich, Tim; and Lynham, Tom (Eds.), *From Here to Here: Stories Inspired By London's Circle Line* (Cyan Books, 2005).
A collection of stories that celebrate the portions of London attached to the Circle line.

Ward, Chris, *The Tube Riders* (AMMFA, 2012).
Futuristic, dystopian London sets the scene, with much of the story set below the city streets.

WEBSITES

www.abandonedstations.org.uk
Search for disused stations by line and depth; lots of photos of the remnants below ground.

www.animalsontheunderground.com
A delightful site showing animals hidden in the London Underground map.

www.diamondgeezer.blogspot.co.uk
London blogger offers lengthy and regular posts with a leaning towards Tube travel and goings on below ground on the transport network.

www.geofftech.co.uk/tube
A serial Tube Challenger tells tales of his record-breaking attempts.

www.london-tubemap.com
A geographically accurate take on today's Tube map.

www.london-underground.blogspot.co.uk
Popular and regularly updated London Underground blog – nothing Tube-related gets past author Annie Mole.

www.ltmcollection.org
The official website for the London Transport Museum; offers a wealth of history about the London Underground.

www.ltmuseumshop.co.uk
The official website for the London Transport Museum shop – offering perfect gifts for the Tube fanatic.

www.metroland.org.uk
A delightful archive of photographs detailing the history of the growth of the Metropolitan Railway's Metro-land.

www.peopleonthetube.tumblr.com
Whatever you do on the Tube, don't fall asleep! You might end up on here…

www.tfl.gov.uk/tube
The official home of the Tube, with a journey planner, service updates and information on planned works.

www.traintimes.org.uk/map/tube
A live map of London detailing the different Tube lines and the locations of trains on the network in approximate real time.

www.underground-history.co.uk
Incredibly informative site focusing on disused stations on the network – with plenty of photos.

www.underlondon.tumblr.com
Picture-led blog focused on the Underground, featuring a host of delights from quotations and signage, to inspired ideas, and quirky and beautiful photographs.

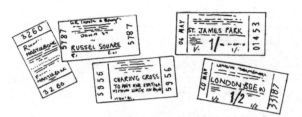

THANK YOU...

Andrew and Phoebe Burton; Charlotte, Nicholas and Alexander Kearns; Joan Hamilton; Lisa Thumwood; Eliza Walsh; Luke Scott; Anna Mills; Olly Thomas; Holly Howe; Christina Dixon; Clare Gowan; Josephine Eaton; Mr K; Caroline Steele; Cyrilene Isaac at TfL; Ajit Chambers of the Old London Underground Company; Zhan Guo of NYU; Abbie, Ellie and Jennifer at Summersdale; Ray Hamilton.

If you're interested in finding out more about our books,
follow us on Twitter: **@Summersdale**

Thanks very much for buying this Summersdale book.

www.summersdale.com

B.T. Tower

camden Market

S

Buckingham Palace

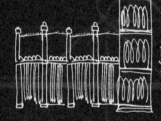

PIC

BIG

BEN

Harrods

Royal Albert Hall